PRESIDENT'S MALARIA INITIATIVE

Angola

Malaria Operational Plan FY 2016

TABLE OF CONTENTS

ABBREVIATIONS and ACRONYMS

ACT	Artemisinin-based combination therapy
ADECOS	Community health worker (*Agentes de Desenvolvimento Communitario e de Saude*)
AL	Artemether-lumefantrine
ANC	Antenatal care
AS-AQ	Artesunate-amodiaquine
BCC	Behavior change communication
CDC	Centers for Disease Control and Prevention
CDCS	Country Development Cooperation Strategy
CECOMA	Central Unit for Procurement and Provision of Medicines and Medical Supplies (*Central de Compras de Medicamentos de Angola*)
DHP	Dihydroartemisinin-piperaquine
DHS	Demographic and Health Survey
DNME	National Directorate of Medicines and Equipment (*Direcção Nacional de Medicamentos e Equipamentos*)
DPS	Provincial Health Directorate (*Direcção Provincial da Saúde*)
EPI	Expanded program on immunization
EPR	Epidemic preparedness and response
FBO	Faith-based organization
FELTP	Field Epidemiology and Laboratory Training Program
FY	Fiscal year
GHI	Global Health Initiative
Global Fund	Global Fund to Fight AIDS, Tuberculosis and Malaria
GRA	Government of Angola
HMIS	Health management information system
iCCM	Integrated community case management
IEC	Information, education and communication
INE	National Institute of Statistics (*Instituto Nacional de Estatística*)
IPTp	Intermittent preventive treatment in pregnant women
IRS	Indoor residual spraying
ITN	Insecticide-treated mosquito net
JICA	Japan International Cooperation Agency
M&E	Monitoring and evaluation
MIP	Malaria in pregnancy
MIS	Malaria indicator survey
MoH	Ministry of Health
MOP	Malaria Operational Plan
NGO	Non-governmental organization
NMCP	National Malaria Control Program
OR	Operational research
PMI	President's Malaria Initiative
PNDS	National Health Development Plan (*Plano Nacional de Desenvolvimento Sanitário*)

QA/QC	Quality assurance/quality control
RBM	Roll Back Malaria
RDT	Rapid diagnostic test
SP	Sulfadoxine-pyrimethamine
TES	Therapeutic Efficacy Study
UNICEF	United Nations Children's Fund
USAID	United States Agency for International Development
USG	United States Government
WHO	World Health Organization

I. EXECUTIVE SUMMARY

When it was launched in 2005, the goal of the President's Malaria Initiative (PMI) was to reduce malaria-related mortality by 50% across 15 high-burden countries in sub-Saharan Africa through a rapid scale-up of four proven and highly effective malaria prevention and treatment measures: insecticide-treated mosquito nets (ITNs); indoor residual spraying (IRS); accurate diagnosis and prompt treatment with artemisinin-based combination therapies (ACTs); and intermittent preventive treatment of pregnant women (IPTp). With the passage of the Tom Lantos and Henry J. Hyde Global Leadership against HIV/AIDS, Tuberculosis, and Malaria Act in 2008, PMI developed a U.S. Government Malaria Strategy for 2009–2014. This strategy included a long-term vision for malaria control in which sustained high coverage with malaria prevention and treatment interventions would progressively lead to malaria-free zones in Africa, with the ultimate goal of worldwide malaria eradication by 2040-2050. Consistent with this strategy and the increase in annual appropriations supporting PMI, four new sub-Saharan African countries and one regional program in the Greater Mekong Subregion of Southeast Asia were added in 2011. The contributions of PMI, together with those of other partners, have led to dramatic improvements in the coverage of malaria control interventions in PMI-supported countries, and all 15 original countries have documented substantial declines in all-cause mortality rates among children less than five years of age.

In 2015, PMI launched the next six-year strategy, setting forth a bold and ambitious goal and objectives. The PMI Strategy 2015-2020 takes into account the progress over the past decade and the new challenges that have arisen. Malaria prevention and control remains a major U.S. foreign assistance objective and PMI's Strategy fully aligns with the U.S. Government's vision of ending preventable child and maternal deaths and ending extreme poverty. It is also in line with the goals articulated in the RBM Partnership's second generation global malaria action plan, *Action and Investment to defeat Malaria (AIM) 2016-2030: for a Malaria-Free World* and WHO's updated *Global Technical Strategy: 2016-2030*. Under the PMI Strategy 2015-2020, the U.S. Government's goal is to work with PMI-supported countries and partners to further reduce malaria deaths and substantially decrease malaria morbidity, towards the long-term goal of elimination.

Angola was selected as a PMI focus country in FY 2005.

This FY 2016 Malaria Operational Plan presents a detailed implementation plan for Angola, based on the strategies of PMI and the National Malaria Control Program (NMCP). It was developed in consultation with the NMCP and with the participation of national and international partners involved in malaria prevention and control in the country. The activities that PMI is proposing to support fit in well with the National Malaria Control strategy and plan and build on investments made by PMI and other partners to improve and expand malaria-related services, including the Global Fund to Fight AIDS, Tuberculosis, and Malaria (Global Fund) malaria grants. This document briefly reviews the current status of malaria control policies and interventions in Angola, describes progress to date, identifies challenges and unmet needs to achieving the targets of the NMCP and PMI, and provides a description of activities that are planned with FY 2016 funding.

The proposed FY 2016 PMI budget for Angola is $27,000,000. PMI will support the following intervention areas with these funds:

Insecticide-treated nets: With the completion of the mass distribution campaign expected in 2016 and decreases in revenue impacting the Government of Angola (GRA) budget, PMI will focus its net distribution efforts in the hyperendemic provinces where nets can be most effective in preventing malaria transmission, and on the most vulnerable populations of children under five years of age and pregnant women. PMI will continue to support transportation of ITNs from the central the provincial levels. PMI will use traditional distribution methods such as ANC clinics for pregnant women and Expanded Programme on Immunization (EPI) for children under five years of age. Furthermore, PMI Angola will engage technical assistance to determine the most cost effective channels for increasing net coverage and to develop a continuous distribution strategy in collaboration with NMCP. PMI may revisit Child Health Days if these are deemed to be an effective outreach channel. BCC will be provided to maximize use of nets where provided.

With FY 2016 funding, PMI will continue its strategic malaria control focus in provinces with hyperendemic malaria transmission, and provide logistics assistance to move the procured nets from the central level to select provinces. PMI will support routine distribution of nets through antenatal care (ANC) for pregnant women and EPI for children under five and possibly additional channels, if appropriate. In addition, PMI will provide technical assistance to help in-country stakeholders implement a continuous distribution strategy (developed with FY 2015 funds) to improve ITN coverage in high burden provinces.

Vector Control: Due to the high cost and low GRA priority, PMI will no longer provide support for implementation of IRS activities. However, PMI will continue to provide technical assistance for entomologic and epidemiologic monitoring in order to determine the effects of IRS withdrawal on the entomologic and epidemiologic setting. This technical assistance is needed due to the minimal entomologic capacity in country and the need to continue to understand how malaria transmission is occurring in Angola and post-IRS settings. There will be continued trainings to improve mosquito identification skills, build local provincial and district capacity to perform mosquito collections, insecticide resistance tests and longitudinal entomological surveillance. Training in mosquito rearing techniques will be focused at sites where mosquito rearing will take place. The technical assistance will include species identification, susceptibility studies and vector density monitoring. Monitoring in Malanje, Huambo, and Cunene will continue monthly at one to two sites per province. PMI will continue to advocate at the national and provincial levels for the GRA to be more engaged and take greater ownership of its entomological monitoring, including salaries and materials for Angolan entomologists and management of the insectary. Technical assistance trips by CDC entomologists will occur to strengthen and oversee the activities that are done in a field setting. PMI will continue to support molecular analysis support for mosquito identification while it continues to work with the MoH to build up their PCR capacity within the country. PMI will also provide the needed supplies and reagents such as field collecting material, entomologic supplies to support Huambo entomology laboratory and insectary, and insecticide resistance testing material to perform these entomologic activities.

With FY 2016 funding, PMI will strategically shift from providing IRS support and technical assistance to developing a greater knowledge of the entomologic map in Angola through entomologic surveillance in select provinces. Entomologic surveillance will include species identification, susceptibility studies, and vector density monitoring. PMI will develop capacity at both the central and provincial levels and work in areas where IRS susceptibility studies were undertaken, as well as in Lunda Norte and Lunda Sul. PMI will continue to advocate at the provincial level for funding for entomological activities and staff, and to emphasize the critical importance of entomological capacity to monitor vector control efforts. Also, PMI will continue to provide molecular analysis using PCR techniques to identify and confirm mosquito species, while capacity is developed and maintained in Angola. For continued support, CDC will provide two technical assistance trips to maintain strides made in entomologic monitoring and insecticide resistance testing at the central level. The support also includes reagents for entomologic testing and other laboratory diagnostic equipment and supplies.

Malaria in pregnancy: The 2011 MIS revealed that only 17.5% of pregnant women declared having taken at least two doses of IPTp during their last pregnancy. Therefore, PMI will continue efforts to increase IPTp rates for the upcoming year. PMI will support the health facilities to continue to strengthen ANC services, maintain support for training and supervision, print revised training manuals, and promote early and regular ANC attendance.

With FY 2016 funding, PMI will continue to collaborate with the NMCP and Reproductive Health Division to strengthen prevention, diagnosis, and treatment of malaria in pregnancy at municipal, health facility, and community levels. The proposed activities are cross cutting with some ITN activities, case management, and behavior change communication (BCC) activities. PMI will support training and supervision of healthcare workers, and dissemination of current policy to provide at least three doses of sulfadoxine-pyrimethamine (SP) at the municipal and facility levels. PMI will develop BCC strategy with appropriate, targeted messages for the community, focusing in particular on rural population with low education. This will include developing and conducting training for outreach workers, improving communication skills, producing materials for distribution to incentivize IPTp and ITN use by identifying and promoting positive behavior. Also, PMI will strengthen malaria in pregnancy services at health facilities through training and regular supervisions of healthcare providers, therefore improving the diagnosis and treatment of malaria in pregnant women. PMI will support routine ITN distribution through ANC.

Case management: Given uncertainties in Global Fund and GRA funding for malaria commodities, and recent nationwide stockouts of malaria commodities, NMCP has requested continued PMI support for malaria commodities procurement, including laboratory diagnostic reagents and supplies not available locally in Angola, rapid diagnostic tests (RDTs), ACTs, and treatments for severe malaria. PMI will procure RDTs and ACTs, but within the context of nationwide stockouts resulting from the Ministry of Health not procuring the commodities it had been expected to, the end of the Global Fund grant, and the inability of PMI alone to fill the enormous gap for ACTs and RDTs, PMI has decided to direct the commodities it procures to be distributed in the highest malaria burden provinces, instead of across all 18 provinces. PMI recognizes that all Angolans deserve access to life-saving commodities. However, in the current context PMI must prioritize the most vulnerable people living in the high-risk areas where PMI hopes to make the most impact in reducing malaria morbidity and mortality. PMI will continue to encourage Angolan government leadership at the national and provincial levels to increase its commitment to malaria control.

Since expansion of access to RDTs and ACTs necessarily involves improving case management at the health facility level, PMI will continue to support training and supervision of healthcare workers and laboratory technicians. Capitalizing on the presence of provincial and municipal malaria supervisors, PMI will work to strengthen their capacity to train and supervise healthcare workers on malaria case management. This will involve training the supervisors on formative supervision and supporting them to be able to conduct regular, scheduled supervisions in health facilities in their areas. Similarly, PMI will support and train provincial-level laboratory supervisors to build their technical capacity to properly conduct trainings and formative supervisions, and provide them logistical support to conduct regular, scheduled supervisions in laboratories in their areas. These activities will be focused in priority provinces, comprising the northern, hyperendemic provinces. PMI supports NMCP's strategy to implement a pilot test of iCCM in the upcoming community health worker program (ADECOS) as a first step to expanding the community health worker program to include malaria case management. Thus, PMI will continue to support piloting integrated community case management (iCCM). Data collected from this pilot program are expected to allow NMCP to advocate for the policy that all community health workers perform malaria diagnosis and treatment in their communities.

With FY 2016 funding, PMI will procure laboratory diagnostic reagents and supplies not available locally in Angola, procure RDTs for the public sector and private sector, procure ASAQ for the public sector, and procure injectable artesunate and intramuscular artemether for treatment of severe malaria. PMI will strengthen malaria case management through training and formative supervision for provincial and health facility health workers, training and formative supervision for provincial and municipal laboratory supervisors to improve malaria diagnostics in the laboratory, and training of trainers at the provincial of laboratory supervisors on conducting formative supervision. PMI will support the GRA's iCCM initiative with ADECOS (community health workers) in select municipalities. PMI will provide technical assistance to support continuation and sustainable transition of private sector case management services activity.

Health systems strengthening and integration: PMI supports a broad array of health system strengthening activities which cut across intervention areas, such as training of health workers, supply chain management and health information systems strengthening, drug quality monitoring, and NMCP capacity building. PMI will continue work to build systems and human capacity for managing and monitoring malaria programs. An emphasis will be placed on strengthening the lower levels of the decentralized health system, to ensure that management improvements have a direct impact on the availability and quality of malaria services.

With FY 2016 funding PMI will improve health information and supervisory systems for malaria as a component of broader systems strengthening approach, finalize and disseminate the new Malaria in Pregnancy Manual, support integrated supervision by NMCP and local health authorities, support the development of municipal operating plans for health, train municipal supervisors on malaria best practices, and improve health information management system (HIMS) capacity at the local level. PMI will continue to support two students from the Field Epidemiology and Laboratory Training Program (FELTP) to focus on malaria activities. PMI will work with national and select provincial counterparts to enhance the annual budget formulation process for malaria commodities, and provide technical assistance to strengthen medium-term planning for sustainable access to these commodities. PMI will support the Malaria Partners' Forum to assist the NMCP and provinces to coordinate malaria partners, and conduct supportive supervision to provincial malaria supervisors to provide them with feedback and assistance.

Behavior Change Communication: Since many Angolans do not have access to public health facilities, improving awareness of malaria at the household level is an especially important element of the malaria control strategy. A key component of this strategy is the implementation of iCCM, which is aimed at reaching the underserved population. Once the ADECOS policy is approved and becomes part of the health system, health promotion will be a key component of community health workers' activities.

PMI plans to focus on the development and roll out of communications materials for mass media and community-based activities, interpersonal communication, pre-season transmission malaria prevention activities, and case management of malaria. Evidence-based messages focused on a target audience will be used and support will be provided to the NMCP to begin to evaluate specific interventions and actual behavior change.

With FY 2016 funding, PMI will support the roll out of the BCC strategy currently under development by engaging malaria forum members, including civil society groups, international partners, private sector and donors. PMI will develop and conduct training for outreach workers, in order to improve communication skills, undertake BCC at the community and facility levels to promote net use and continue to build a net culture, and use BCC to improve prevention of malaria in pregnancy at the community level, through promotion of ANC attendance and education on the importance of ITN use and receiving at least three doses of IPTp.

Monitoring and evaluation: PMI will continue to support malaria M&E within the framework of the National Malaria M&E Plan described in the National Strategic Plan for Malaria Control (2011-2015). Available funding will be targeted towards improving the country's M&E capacity, data quality assurance, and using data for decision making.

With FY 2016 funding, PMI will continue bi-annual End-use verification/monitoring of commodity availability and use at health facility level, support CDC TDYs to provide M&E assistance to the NMCP and in-country partners, expand pilot of Health Management Information System (HMIS) database from Huambo to select municipalities in hyperendemic areas, and support a third Therapeutic Efficacy Study (TES) to be conducted in the three sites established in 2015 (Benguela, Zaire, and Lunda Sul).

Operational research (OR): PMI plans to support a qualitative study of malaria health seeking behavior and prevention practices in Southeast Asian migrant worker population, many of whom come from malaria endemic and drug-resistant areas. The size of this population in Angola is estimated to be 400,000, considered to be the largest concentrated population of Southeast Asians in Africa.

II. STRATEGY

1. Introduction

When it was launched in 2005, the goal of PMI was to reduce malaria-related mortality by 50% across 15 high-burden countries in sub-Saharan Africa through a rapid scale-up of four proven and highly effective malaria prevention and treatment measures: insecticide-treated mosquito nets (ITNs); indoor residual spraying (IRS); accurate diagnosis and prompt treatment with artemisinin-based combination therapies (ACTs); and intermittent preventive treatment of pregnant women (IPTp). With the passage of the Tom Lantos and Henry J. Hyde Global Leadership against HIV/AIDS, Tuberculosis, and Malaria Act in 2008, PMI developed a U.S. Government Malaria Strategy for 2009–2014. This strategy included a long-term vision for malaria control in which sustained high coverage with malaria prevention and treatment interventions would progressively lead to malaria-free zones in Africa, with the ultimate goal of worldwide malaria eradication by 2040-2050. Consistent with this strategy and the increase in annual appropriations supporting PMI, four new sub-Saharan African countries and one regional program in the Greater Mekong Subregion of Southeast Asia were added in 2011. The contributions of PMI, together with those of other partners, have led to dramatic improvements in the coverage of malaria control interventions in PMI-supported countries, and all 15 original countries have documented substantial declines in all-cause mortality rates among children less than five years of age.

In 2015, PMI launched the next six-year strategy, setting forth a bold and ambitious goal and objectives. The PMI Strategy 2015-2020 takes into account the progress over the past decade and the new challenges that have arisen. Malaria prevention and control remains a major U.S. foreign assistance objective and PMI's Strategy fully aligns with the U.S. Government's vision of ending preventable child and maternal deaths and ending extreme poverty. It is also in line with the goals articulated in the draft Roll Back Malaria (RBM) Partnership's *Action and Investment to Defeat Malaria, 2016-2030* and WHO's *Global Technical Strategy for Malaria, 2016-2030*. Under the PMI Strategy 2015-2020, the U.S. Government's goal is to work with PMI-supported countries and partners to further reduce malaria deaths and substantially decrease malaria morbidity, towards the long-term goal of elimination.

Angola was selected as a PMI focus countries in FY 2005.

This FY 2016 Malaria Operational Plan presents a detailed implementation plan for Angola based on the strategies of PMI and the National Malaria Control Program (NMCP) strategy. It was developed in consultation with the NMCP and with the participation of national and international partners involved in malaria prevention and control in the country. The activities that PMI is proposing to support fit in well with the National Malaria Control strategy and plan and build on investments made by PMI and other partners to improve and expand malaria-related services, including the Global Fund to Fight AIDS, Tuberculosis, and Malaria (Global Fund) malaria grants. This document briefly reviews the current status of malaria control policies and interventions in Angola, describes progress to date, identifies challenges and unmet needs to achieving the targets of the NMCP and PMI, and provides a description of activities that are planned with FY 2016 funding.

2. Malaria situation in Angola

According to the preliminary results from the 2014 population census conducted by the *Instituto Nacional de Estatística* (INE) (National Institute of Statistics of Angola), Angola has an estimated population of 24,383,301, of which 52% are women and 48% are men. The majority of the population (62%) is urban. The country is divided into 18 provinces, 165 municipalities, and 532 communes.

Significant progress has been made in the fight against malaria in Angola, and data from the 2011 Malaria Indicator Survey (MIS) show an almost 40% decline in parasitemia among children under five years of age from the 2006/7 MIS (from 21% to 13.5%). According to the 2011 MIS, the mortality rate for children under five years of age has fallen by 23% over the last five years, and it is currently estimated at 91 deaths per 1,000 live births.

Nonetheless, malaria continues to be a major health problem and is the principal cause of morbidity and mortality in Angola. Malaria accounts for 35% of curative care demand, 35% of mortality in children, 40% of pre-natal mortality, 25% of maternal morbidity, and causes 60% of hospital admissions in children under five years of age and 10% of admissions of pregnant women (PNDS 2013, annex 4). Furthermore, malaria is a leading cause of low birth weight, and anemia due to malaria is a major cause of morbidity and mortality in both children and pregnant women.

In 2014, there were 3,180,021 cases (confirmed and suspected) of malaria reported in the public sector in Angola, with 5,714 deaths (NMCP 2014). The majority of cases of malaria are caused by *Plasmodium falciparum* (87%), with a portion of cases caused by *P. vivax*, *P. malariae*, and *P. ovale* (estimated at 7%, 3%, and 3%, respectively).[1] It is believed that there are five anopheline species responsible for malaria transmission in the country: *Anopheles gambiae* s.s., *An. funestus*, *An. melas* (in coastal areas), *An. arabiensis* and *An. pharaoensis* (in southern unstable meoendemic areas). Further entomology studies are needed to confirm the vector species in the country.

The entire Angolan population is at risk for malaria, but there is significant heterogeneity in transmission, with hyperendemicity in the northeast provinces: Cabinda, Uige, Kuanza Norte, Malanje, Lunda Norte, and Lunda Sul. In the north, the peak malaria transmission season extends from March to May, with a secondary peak in October-November. The central and coastal provinces are largely mesoendemic with stable transmission: Zaire, Luanda, Kwanza Sul, Benguela, Huambo, Bie, and Moxico. The four southern provinces bordering Namibia have highly seasonal transmission and are prone to epidemics (see Figure 1, below). Angola is party to two trans-border initiatives for malaria control: the Trans-Kunene (with Namibia) and the Trans-Zambeze (with Botswana, Namibia, Zambia, and Zimbabwe). Angola is a member of the "Elimination 8" countries (along with Botswana, Mozambique, Namibia, Swaziland, South Africa, Zambia, and Zimbabwe).

---

[1] Fortes, F et al. (2014) *Estudo do Parasita da Malaria em Angola em Assintomaticos, por Tecnicas Comparativas de Microscopia Optica e Biologia Molecular.* (The estimation of P. vivax is 2.5-7%.)

Figure 1: Malaria Transmission in Angola

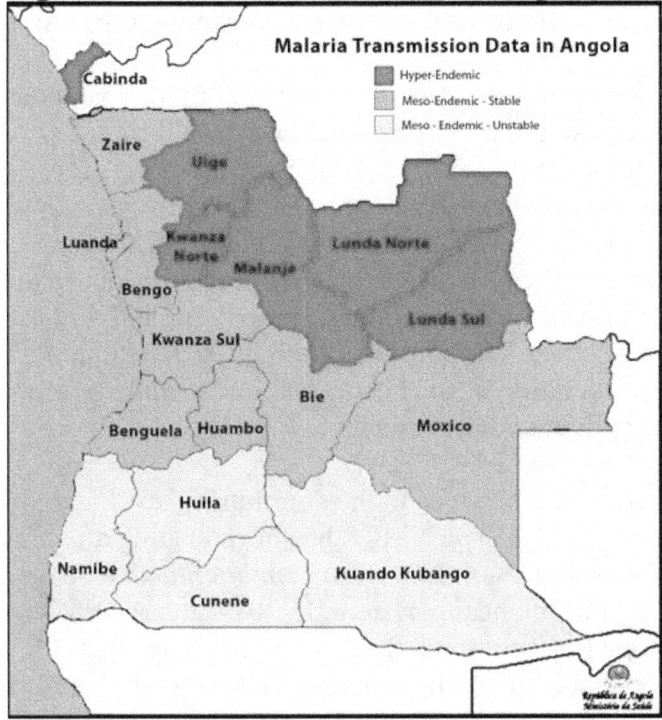

3. Country health system delivery structure and Ministry of Health (MoH) organization

The government has been investing in health infrastructure and working to expand the health network, emphasizing primary care facilities. It is estimated that about 45% of the population has access to public health facilities (PDNS, 2013). However, there are major disparities among provinces in terms of public investment levels, and people travel longer distances to access health facilities in the easternmost provinces. Furthermore, there is notable disparity between urban and rural inhabitants' access to care. Service delivery is also affected by unbalanced distribution of human resources, stockouts of commodities, and poor infrastructure. Contributing factors to low access to public healthcare include cultural beliefs and reliance on traditional healers and preference of purchasing medicine from private drug sellers without medical consultation.

The Angolan National Health System has three levels of care: primary care, in which basic care is provided through health posts, health centers, and municipal hospitals; secondary care, in which care is provided through general (provincial) hospitals; and tertiary care, in which specialized care is provided through central hospitals in the capital city of Luanda. The public health network is composed of a total of 2,356 health units, including: (i) 1,650 health posts; (ii) 331 health centers; (iii) 43 maternal and child health centers; (iv) 165 municipal hospitals; (v) 25 provincial hospitals; (vi) 20 central/national hospitals, of which 15 are in Luanda, 2 in Benguela, 2 in Huambo, and 1 in Huila; (vii) 39 national level health facilities; and (viii) 83 non-classified health facilities. While the Government of Angola (GRA) has prioritized increasing human resources for health (and the number of doctors tripled between 2005 and 2009), there is still a critical shortage and inequitable distribution of health workers. For example, in 2009 there were an estimated 18 doctors per 100,000 persons and 85% of health workers worked in urban areas.

The MoH currently has four levels of administration: the national, provincial, municipal, and health facility. The central level includes the National Directorate of Public Health of the Ministry of Health (where the NMCP is located), where national guidelines and norms are elaborated, adapted, or adopted, and the national technical direction is set. The provincial level, which includes the *Direcção Provincial da Saúde* (Provincial Health Directorate [DPS]), is responsible for coordinating all health activities in the province and providing oversight to the general (provincial) hospitals. The municipal level provides technical and operational directives to municipal hospitals, local health centers, and posts. The administration of each health facility provides direct supervision for the day-to-day operation of the health unit and health staff, but each facility depends on the municipality for budget and procurement.

The government recognizes the need to extend health services to the community level and to adopt integrated community case management (iCCM). The NMCP has been leading a process to develop a community approach using *Agentes de Desenvolvimento Communitario e de Saude* (ADECOS) (community health workers) as part of the health system. In 2014, the ADECOS national policy framework was jointly developed by the Angolan Ministry of Territorial Administration and the MoH, and has been approved by both ministries. The next step is for the policy to be presented to the council of Angolan ministries for final approval and adoption and implementation. Currently, the main objectives of the CHWs are to increase awareness in the community of health prevention interventions, such as basic malaria prevention activities (e.g., use of ITNs, early treatment seeking, and compliance with diagnostic outcomes), as well as vaccination, improved sanitation, access to safe water, etc. Implementation was scheduled to begin in 2015 in 18 municipalities in 7 provinces, with a target of 1,080 CHWs trained initially (14,100 by 2017). The planned three-month curriculum includes training on providing some basic services including testing with RDTs and administering ACTs. Severe cases are to be referred to the nearest health facility. CHWs will be linked to municipal health centers, where integrated health teams will be responsible for performing routine supervision. Salaries and operational costs are to be covered by the Ministry of Territorial Administration. At the time of writing, this process is still ongoing, with the policy yet to be adopted.

Since the late 1990s, the GRA has embarked upon various degrees of administrative and more recently, fiscal, decentralization. The law now grants municipal governments the authority to budget, manage, and implement their own pools of funds. In an attempt to improve public services, in 2012 the GRA transferred over $400 million dollars to municipal governments, mostly to carry out health services. Next to be decentralized are water and education services, where funds will be allocated directly to the municipalities. In 2015, 12.96% of the overall GRA budget went to the social sector, with 5.5% for health.

In 2013, the GRA approved the *Plano Nacional de Desenvolvimento Sanitário* (National Health Development Plan [PNDS]), which outlines the strategy to improve the health system from 2012-2025. This strategy has been costed with technical support from PMI. All municipalities have developed municipal health development strategies which are funded through the direct funds they receive from the Ministry of Finance ($2 million annually), enabling them to plan health activities independently of the provincial level.

The NMCP is composed of a core central technical group at the national level, including specialists responsible for epidemiology, parasitological, entomology, case management, malaria in pregnancy, monitoring and evaluation, and behavior change communication as well as for administration and fund management. In addition, there are 18 provincial malaria control supervisors (typically health technicians) and malaria municipal supervisors in the municipal health directorate staff who are responsible for institutional support in planning, implementing and managing malaria activities at these levels. Until 2014, the Global Fund had seconded one provincial official for malaria in each of the 18 provinces to support the malaria provincial supervisors. Funding for this position has ended and the GRA is in the process of integrating these personnel into the government-funded health system. Entomology core teams (34 technicians trained in entomology) have been created at provincial and municipal levels to conduct routine entomologic monitoring. A national insectary has been installed in the province of Huambo. A consultative reference group, the National Technical Committee for Malaria, has been constituted to provide technical assistance to the NMCP.

4. National malaria control strategy

The general objective of the National Malaria Strategic Plan (2016-2020) is to reduce by 60% morbidity and mortality related to malaria by 2020, from 2012 baseline figures. The strategy includes the following objectives and targets:

Prevention of Malaria: The NMCP's strategy for malaria prevention has four main components: ITNs, prevention of malaria in pregnancy, spraying (indoor and outdoor), and larviciding. (1) The GRA strategy calls for two approaches for ITN distribution: mass campaign distribution to achieve universal coverage and routine distribution to maintain coverage. At the time of writing, the rolling mass distribution campaign, which started in 2013, was still underway. Routine distribution of ITNs occurs through the following channels: (i) distribution at antenatal care clinics (ANC) and the expanded program for immunization (EPI), and (ii) outreach services for communities with no or little access to health services such as mobile municipal health units and municipal health days. (2) In addition to distributing ITNs to pregnant women to help prevent malaria in pregnancy, national policy calls for provision of IPTp with sulfadoxine-pyramethamine (SP) at all health units with ANC services. The target is that by the end of 2020, at least 80% of pregnant women with access to ANC and targeted for IPTp receive at least three doses of IPTp with SP. (3) The NMCP strategy calls for indoor and outdoor residual spraying to be implemented in targeted areas of epidemic risks and low transmission. (4) Larviciding is fully financed by GRA with technical support from the Cuban government.

Malaria Case Management: In accordance with WHO guidelines, Angola's strategic plan recommends that all suspected cases of malaria be diagnosed parasitologically, using either microscopy or RDTs. Only positively confirmed malaria cases should be treated with an ACT. The country has three alternative first-line ACT treatments: artesunate-amodiaquine (AS-AQ), artemeter-lumefantrine (AL), and dihydroartemisinin+piperaquine (DHA-PQ). National treatment guidelines for severe malaria recommend (in order of preference) injectable artesunate, intramuscular artemether, and injectable quinine. Injectable quinine continues to be the most commonly used treatment for severe malaria nationwide, and is also commonly used for treatment of simple malaria, particularly during stockouts of ACTs. Currently, malaria case management is only provided at the health facility level. However, the NMCP plans to extend it to the community level, pending ministerial approval of the community case management policy. PMI has been supporting a pilot program to provide quality malaria diagnosis and treatment at a network of private pharmacies in Huambo and Uige Provinces; the government plans to expand this private sector approach to other provinces with proposed Global Fund support.

Monitoring and Evaluation and Epidemiologic Surveillance: The NMCP has developed a Monitoring and Evaluating (M&E) Plan described in the National Strategic Plan for Malaria Control (2011-2015). At national level, the NMCP has a National Focal Point for M&E. Morbidity and mortality data are collected from the health facilities and administrative and managerial levels, integrating not only malaria related data but also data on logistics and essential malaria drugs provision and consumption. At each province, there is a malaria supervisor. At the municipal level, there is a malaria municipal supervisor who regularly collects data and transmits them to the national program, through the provincial level.

The GRA is working to strengthen its epidemiology surveillance system. The National Epidemiological Surveillance System collects weekly reports on clinically diagnosed cases of malaria from the four epidemic-prone provinces in the south— Namibe, Huila, Cunene, and Cuando Cubango. However, since not all districts report on a regular basis and there are delays in releasing reports to the NMCP, these weekly data are currently of limited value for detecting and containing malaria epidemics. Nonetheless, the strategy's target is that by the end of 2020, 100% of eligible municipalities of the southern provinces of Angola (Cunene, Huambo, Huila, Cuando Cubango and Namibe) will be at the pre-elimination phase.

Procurement and supply management: The National Programme of Essential Drugs revised the content of national essential drugs kits both for health posts and for health centers in 2012. Anti-malarial drugs, including ACTs, rectal artesunate, and SP are delivered to health facilities through these drug kits; RDTs and injectable artesunate are still individually distributed. The number of kits received by each health facility and the frequency of reception are based on consumption. Municipal, provincial and central (national) hospitals are accorded budgets and are responsible for procurement of their health commodity needs.

5. Updates in the strategy section

- Shift in geographic scope to focus implementation of prevention and case management activities, as well as distribution of commodities, in hyper-endemic provinces in the north and east, while maintaining strategic surveillance, monitoring and evaluation, and health systems strengthening investments at the national level.
- Continuation of universal coverage distribution campaign (though anticipated to conclude in 2015, will continue through 2016)
- End of consolidated Global Fund Round 7 and Round 10 grant (March 2015) and submission of new Global Fund concept note (April 30, 2015)

- Development of new iCCM approach using *Agentes de Desenvolvimento Communitario e de Saude* (ADECOS) (community health workers)

6. Integration, collaboration, and coordination

Funding

Funding of malaria control in Angola is provided by the GRA, private partners such as the ExxonMobil Foundation and Chevron, and PMI. While the GRA has historically also received contributions from the Global Fund, World Bank, WHO, UNICEF, Japan International Cooperation Agency (JICA), the Cuban Government, the Spanish Cooperation, the GAVI Alliance, and private partners, PMI is currently the only significant bilateral donor for malaria in Angola. The consolidated Global Fund Round 7 and Round 10 granted ended in March 2015; Angola has submitted a concept note proposal for the new funding model, which was under review at the time of writing.

The overall Angolan budget for health in 2015 was approximately $2.5 billion, with the NMCP receiving approximately $4.1 million. These funds are used for commodity procurement, larviciding, training and capacity building of health personnel, and general operational costs. National hospitals in Luanda, the provincial hospitals, and some municipal and provincial governments receive budgets directly from the GRA, which also contribute to malaria prevention and treatment. In addition, the GRA has made available $2 million per year to each municipal government for health programs, including malaria.

Private Sector

Since the launch of PMI in Angola in 2006, the ExxonMobil Foundation has contributed $6 million to PMI to support the scale up of ACTs, IPTp, and malaria diagnostics, as well as capacity building and health systems strengthening at health facility, municipal, and provincial levels through the PMI-supported USAID Angola NGO-strengthening project. This project was implemented by five non-governmental organizations (NGOs) and faith-based organizations (FBOs).

NMCP Coordination

The NMCP works in close collaboration with other departments at the health directorate, such as Reproductive Health and Maternal and Child Health, on implementation of malaria in pregnancy interventions and Integrated Management of Childhood Illness (IMCI). There is a continued effort to strengthen working relationships within these departments to coordinate efforts and maximize resources.

The Malaria Partners Forum, made up of civil society and other interested partners focused on malaria, was created in 2007 in order to help the NMCP coordinate partners' activities and minimize duplication of efforts and resources. The forum was originally under the leadership of PSI, the founding president. In 2012, an election resulted in new executive leadership, comprised of *Ajuda de Desenvolvimento de Povo para Povo* (ADPP) as president, Chevron and a network of journalists as vice presidents, and technical advisory members. Currently, there are about 100 members, including the NMCP, PMI, WHO, UNICEF, local and international NGOs and FBOs, bilateral and multilateral organizations, Angolan military forces, and private sector companies. The Malaria Partners Forum is also present in some provinces, but coordination of malaria activities at provincial level varies from province to province. In 2013, the Forum was able to double the funding it received by leveraging resources from the ExxonMobil Foundation and others.

Within USG
PMI contributes 65% of the budget for health activities within the USAID Angola Mission and contributes to a number of integrated programs. PMI supported the NMCP in the revitalization and decentralization process, mainly through the USAID integrated health systems strengthening NGO strengthening projects. The integrated program assists health managers at the central and provincial levels to set budgets and track progress against them. Both projects have been working with the NMCP to develop or adopt guidelines and with the municipal leadership to develop administrative, financial, and technical capacity to ensure improved access and quality of all health services, including malaria. In 2015, PMI, along with PEPFAR and other partners, made significant financial and technical contributions to the Demographic and Health Survey (DHS).

7. PMI goal, objectives, strategic areas, and key indicators

Under the PMI Strategy 2015-2020, the U.S. Government's goal is to work with PMI-supported countries and partners to further reduce malaria deaths and substantially decrease malaria morbidity, towards the long-term goal of elimination. Building upon the progress to date in PMI-supported countries, PMI will work with NMCPs and partners to accomplish the following objectives by 2020:

1. Reduce malaria mortality by one-third from 2015 levels in PMI-supported countries, achieving a greater than 80% reduction from PMI's original 2000 baseline levels.

2. Reduce malaria morbidity in PMI-supported countries by 40% from 2015 levels.

3. Assist at least five PMI-supported countries to meet the World Health Organization's (WHO) criteria for national or sub-national pre-elimination.[2]

These objectives will be accomplished by emphasizing five core areas of strategic focus:
1. Achieving and sustaining scale of proven interventions
2. Adapting to changing epidemiology and incorporating new tools
3. Improving countries' capacity to collect and use information
4. Mitigating risk against the current malaria control gains
5. Building capacity and health systems towards full country ownership

To track progress toward achieving and sustaining scale of proven interventions (area of strategic focus #1), PMI will continue to track the key indicators recommended by the Roll Back Malaria Monitoring and Evaluation Reference Group (RBM MERG) as listed below:

---

[2] http://whqlibdoc.who.int/publications/2007/9789241596084_eng.pdf

- Proportion of households with at least one ITN
- Proportion of households with at least one ITN for every two people
- Proportion of children under five years old who slept under an ITN the previous night
- Proportion of pregnant women who slept under an ITN the previous night
- Proportion of households in targeted districts protected by IRS
- Proportion of children under five years old with fever in the last two weeks for whom advice or treatment was sought
- Proportion of children under five with fever in the last two weeks who had a finger or heel stick
- Proportion receiving an ACT among children under five years old with fever in the last two weeks who received any antimalarial drugs
- Proportion of women who received two or more doses of IPTp for malaria during ANC visits during their last pregnancy

8. Progress on coverage/impact indicators to date

A nationwide MIS was conducted between November 2006 and April 2007 with PMI and Global Fund support. This was the first nationwide health survey in more than 20 years in Angola. At the time, ACT and IPTp implementation had only just begun, so the figures reported for the proportion of children under five years of age receiving an ACT and the proportion of pregnant women receiving two doses of IPTp can be considered accurate baselines for PMI. In the case of ITNs, where a large-scale campaign in seven provinces had occurred several months prior to the survey, families interviewed were asked specifically when they had received their bed nets and an adjustment was made in the calculations to take campaign nets into account in estimating the baseline ownership of ITNs.

In 2011, PMI contributed to a second nationwide MIS with an expanded sample size to provide up-to-date information on progress in malaria prevention and treatment activities. Another MIS was planned for 2015, following the national census of 2014. However, a DHS—that will incorporate key malaria indicators— is to be conducted instead. An MIS is planned for 2018. The results for the major indicators used by PMI include the baseline MIS of 2006/7 and the 2011 MIS outlined in the table below:

Table 1: Key Malaria Indicators in Angola

Indicator	2006–2007 MIS	2011 MIS
% Households with at least one ITN	28%*	35%
% Children under five who slept under an ITN the previous night	18%	26%
% Pregnant women who slept under an ITN the previous night	22%	26%
% Children under five years old with fever in the last two weeks who received treatment with an ACT within 24 hours of onset of fever	2%	12%
% Women who received two or more doses of IPTp during their last pregnancy in the last two years	3%	18%

*The estimated PMI baseline before the 2006 measles-ITN mass campaign was 11%.

The table below shows parasitemia at baseline in 2006/2007 MIS compared with 2011 MIS, and demonstrates an almost 40% reduction in parasitemia from 21% to 13.5%.

Table 2: Malaria Parasitemia in Angola

Malaria Transmission Zones	% Parasitemia 2006/2007*	% Parasitemia 2011
Hyperendemic: Cabinda, Uige, Kuanza Norte, Malanje, Lunda Norte, and Lunda Sul	31%	25%
Mesoendemic stable: Zaire, Luanda, Kwanza Sul, Benguela, Huambo, Bie, and Moxico	26%	15%
Mesoendemic unstable: Namibe, Huila, Cunene, Kuando Kubango	21%	9%
Luanda (city)	6%	2%
Total (nationally)	21%	14%

*The 2006/7 figures listed here are from the 2011 MIS report and are different than those published in the 2006/7 MIS (erroneous denominator used in 2006/7 report).

All-cause under-five mortality decreased from 118 deaths per 1,000 live births in 2001-2006 to 91 deaths per 1,000 live births in 2011. This represents a reduction of under-five mortality by 23%.

9. Other relevant evidence on progress

An evaluation of the impact of malaria control interventions on all-cause mortality of children under five years of age in Angola was finalized in September 2014.[3] It found that despite major infrastructure problems caused by the civil war that ended in 2002, progress was made in rolling out some malaria control interventions, evidenced by the increases in ITN ownership and use and IPTp in particular, between 2006/7 and 2011. However, it is unlikely that the overall changes in the coverage of malaria control interventions in 2011 were high enough to impact all-cause mortality of children at a national level. Malaria parasitemia and mortality in children under five years of age decreased nationally during the evaluation period, shown by both the MIS and the Health Management Information System (HMIS); declines in Huambo Province provide an example of this also occurring at the sub-national level. However, larger all-cause mortality of children decreases prior to 2006–2008 are likely due to other contextual factors, such as the end of the civil war, increases in GDP, and childhood vaccination coverage. Despite the overall low coverage of ITNs in 2011, multiple logistic regression analysis showed that household ITN ownership was protective of malaria parasitemia among children under five years of age under programmatic conditions. Therefore, if the implementation of malaria control interventions were to be further scaled-up and sustained in Angola, there is likely to be a larger decline in all-cause childhood mortality nationwide in the future.

10. Challenges and opportunities

The GRA has financial resources to contribute to malaria control and prevention, as well as other important health priorities. Within the framework of the National Health Development Plan, the GRA is costing program areas and allocating more resources to disease prevention. These resources, in conjunction with the process of decentralization, afford an opportunity for the government, especially at the municipal levels, to assume more ownership and financial responsibility for its malaria control program. However, within the context of the drop in oil prices in 2014-2015 and its detrimental impact on Angola's economy, budget allocations for health and malaria were decreased. The Ministry of Health did not purchase the commodities, as they had promised, leading to stockouts of ACTs, rapid diagnostic tests (RDTs), and SP (sulfadoxine-pyrimethamine). Given these nationwide stockouts and the lack of other donors, PMI cannot cover the major gaps throughout the country and thus will distribute PMI-procured commodities in the high-burden provinces where PMI is supporting implementation activities. Furthermore, human resource capacity continues to be a major constraint and challenge in Angola. Continued training and technical assistance to build human resources and strengthen health systems, accompanied by gradual, measured steps toward transition, remain a priority. PMI will continue to advocate to the Ministry of Health at the national and provincial levels to increase its commitment to malaria control and take greater ownership for its program.

---

[3] Evaluation of the impact of malaria control interventions on all-cause mortality in children under 5-years of age in Angola. *Angola Malaria Impact Evaluation Group.*

III. OPERATIONAL PLAN

PMI's strategy for Angola supports most of the NMCP's strategic goals and priorities and complements the efforts of the GRA and other partners. PMI prioritizes malaria prevention and case management and supports capacity building at all levels of the health system. PMI does not support larviciding or outdoor spraying. Due to high costs, low overall impact, and other GRA priorities, PMI has transitioned from implementation support for indoor residual spraying to technical assistance and entomological monitoring. This decision was affected by the costs for covering a small percentage (7%) of the population (MIS 2011). In addition, the NMCP demonstrated that IRS was not a priority by not allocating any of its own funding for the IRS program.

With FY 2016 funding, PMI will focus support for high-impact malaria treatment and prevention activities in areas with high malaria transmission (Uige, Cuanza Norte, Lunda Norte, Lunda Sul, Malanje, Zaire), while continuing surveillance activities in the areas of lower transmission in the southern part of the country and Luanda. In line with USAID Angola Country's Development Cooperation Strategy (CDCS), PMI will continue to emphasize capacity building and health systems strengthening across its interventions and identify opportunities to provide demand-driven technical assistance to the GRA. For example, PMI will continue to build the capacity of the MoH to provide high quality malaria treatment services, conduct entomological and epidemiological surveillance, procure quality-assured antimalarial commodities, and manage its supply chain for health products.

With FY 2016 funding, PMI plans to strengthen and improve service delivery through continuing to build capacity of the NMCP and to:

- Ensure correct and consistent use of ITNs and nurture a net culture after the mass distribution net campaign by supporting BCC and strengthening GRA systems for continuous distribution;
- Scale up entomologic monitoring to inform vector control strategies;
- Improve quality of malaria diagnosis and treatment;
- Increase access to and demand for parasite-based malaria diagnosis and treatment based on results in the public, private, and community arenas;
- Strengthen national-, provincial-, municipal-, and health facility-level technical capacity, as well as local NGO and FBO capacity;
- Improving malaria disease surveillance to provide evidence-based data to inform the malaria control strategy; and
- Monitor program implementation to ensure investments are delivering expected results.

1. Insecticide-treated nets

NMCP/PMI objectives
The NMCP's objectives for ITNs are to achieve universal coverage (i.e., providing one ITN for every two people) through a rolling mass distribution campaign, and to maintain ownership through routine distribution to pregnant women and children under five through ANC and EPI.

The government promotes use and maintenance of ITNs through information, education and communication/behavior change communication (IEC/BCC) messaging in use, care, and repair of nets. The NMCP has incorporated routine monitoring of durability into the national strategy and PMI supports this monitoring in order to determine the performance levels of ITNs. By the end of 2020, the government's target is that at least 80% of the target population uses an adequate preventive measure (i.e., at least 80% of households have at least one ITN for every two people in the household; 80% of people have slept under an ITN the previous night; and 80% of children under five and pregnant have slept under an ITN the previous night).

PMI supports the government's objectives through: procurement and distribution of ITNs from central to provincial levels; support of routine distribution and national campaigns; and BCC messaging to support the burgeoning net culture.

Progress since PMI was launched

Since 2006, over 14 million nets have been distributed in the country through various partners. Multiple partners including the GRA, PMI, Global Fund, UNICEF, UNITAID, JICA, Malaria No More, the ExxonMobil Foundation, and PSI have supported procurement and distribution of ITNs. In addition, there are nets available in the commercial sector for full price. PMI has procured approximately 6 million ITNs and distributed approximately 1.8 million ITNs procured by other partners since 2006. Between 2010 and 2013, 5,058,666 nets were procured and distributed through Global Fund Rounds 7 and 10, the GRA, PMI, JICA, and Exxon Mobil. Distribution has been accompanied by strong BCC messaging to build and support a growing net culture in Angola.

In 2011, an MIS was carried out in Angola, which provided updates on malaria control efforts in Angola. Key findings were:
- Net ownership increase from 11% in 2006 to 35% in 2011 with considerable usage among vulnerable populations;
- 26% of all children under five years slept under an ITN the previous night;
- 61% of all children under five years slept under an ITN, among households with at least one ITN;
- 26% of all pregnant women slept under an ITN the night prior to the survey;
- 68% of pregnant women in households with an ITN slept under an ITN

Progress during the last 12-18 months

For the universal coverage campaign (2013-2015), 7,953,812 nets were procured by the GRA and donors and distributed in 144 municipalities in 16 provinces. In support of this campaign, PMI procured and distributed nets in FY 2013 (900,000) and FY 2014 (950,000). Furthermore, with the ending of the Global Fund grant, PMI provided funds and technical assistance for the distribution of 324,000 Global Fund nets in Huambo, with PMI-procured ITNs covering the rest of the province. At the time of writing, universal coverage has been reached in six provinces (Bengo, Bie, Cabinda, Lunda Norte, Lunda Sul, and Namibe) and partial coverage has been achieved in Uige, while distribution is ongoing in Huambo. Global Fund supported BCC through for mass media campaigns during the mass distribution.

Since the campaign is not yet complete, at the request of the NMCP, PMI is reprogramming FY 2015 funds from support of routine distribution in 9 provinces to continuing support the universal coverage campaign with procurement and distribution of 1.5 million nets in Cunene and Cuanza Sul. Robust BCC messaging will accompany at the local level of distribution. It is expected that the universal coverage campaign will be completed in early 2016.

In April 2014, PMI conducted a continuous distribution workshop in order to introduce the concepts and tools for planning and design of continuous distribution of ITNs to the NMCP and partners, and to train on the use of these tools to support the development of a continuous distribution strategy. It was recommended that Angola complete its mass ITN distributions before using proposed channels for continuous distribution to help improve and sustain ITN coverage over time. The overall need for target populations (pregnant women and children under five years of age) for 2016 is approximately 2.3 million nets. In its concept note application to Global Fund, Angola has requested 6 million nets for 2016 and 2017 (3 million per year). These ITNs will be distributed via continuous distribution channels.

Durability monitoring began in 2011 in Uige and Kwanza Sul Provinces. Two years of field data collection were concluded in 2013. Though the standard life of an ITN is three years, only two years of data were collected because of NMCP plans to distribute additional ITNs in areas of monitoring prior to the third year of data collection, which would have biased the evaluation. Household surveys collected data on attrition, physical durability, and use, care, and repair as well as socio-economic status were collected in the field. Physical inspection to count whole quantity and measure hole size was also conducted. Samples were transported to the CDC in Atlanta, Georgia for analysis of bioefficacy and insecticide content. The WHO Cone bioassays to measure bioefficacy were completed in late 2014, and the insecticide content using high-performance liquid chromatography (HPLC) was completed in early 2015. The analysis of the data for the bioassays and HPLC results will be performed mid-2015 and a final report will be provided before the end of 2015.

Commodity gap analysis

Table 3. ITN Gap Analysis

Calendar Year	2015	2016	2017
Total Targeted Population	25,041,650	25,717,775	26,412,155
Continuous Distribution Needs			
Channel #1: ANC (*0.052)	1,302,166	1,337,324	1,373,432
Channel #2: EPI (*0.048)	1,201,999	1,234,453	1,267,783
Estimated Total Need for Continuous	2,504,165	2,571,777	2,641,215
Mass Distribution Needs			
Estimated Total Need for Campaign (Ongoing rolling mass campaign)	3,238,986	3,634,856	5,016,890
Total Calculated Need: Routine and Campaign	**5,743,151**	**6,206,633**	**7,658,105**
Partner Contributions			
ITNs carried over from previous year	514,689	187,350	
ITNs from MoH**	1,200,000	1,500,000	1,300,000
ITNs from Global Fund Round 10	2,810,812		
ITNs from other donors (JICA)	455,000		
ITNs planned with PMI funding	950,000	1,400,000	1,500,000
Total ITNs Available	**5,930,501**	**3,087,350**	**2,750,000**
Total ITN Surplus (Gap)	**187,349**	**(3,119,283)**	**(4,858,105)**

*Data was collected from PMI team correspondence, the FY 2014 & FY 2015 MOPs, and the Global Fund Concept Note submission from Angola; population numbers were collected from the 2014 Angola census with a 2.7% annual population suspected increase
**Given the current financial crisis in Angola and lack of movement on MoH procurements to date, it is unlikely that these contributions will be forthcoming. Thus, the ITN gap will most likely be even higher than estimated.

Plans and justification

With the completion of the mass distribution campaign expected in 2016 and decreases in revenue impacting the Angolan Government budget, PMI will focus its net distribution efforts in the hyperendemic provinces where nets can be most effective in preventing malaria transmission and on the most vulnerable populations of children under five years of age and pregnant women. PMI will continue to support transportation of ITNs from the central the provincial levels. PMI will use traditional distribution methods such as ANC clinics for pregnant women and EPI for children under five years of age. Furthermore, PMI Angola will engage technical assistance to determine the most cost effective channels for increasing net coverage and to develop a continuous distribution strategy in collaboration with NMCP, PMI will explore other potential distribution channels, which might include Child Health Days. BCC will be provided to maximize use of nets where provided.

Proposed activities with FY 2016 funding: ($9,805,000)
1. PMI will procure 1.45 million ITNs to be distributed via routine distribution in select provinces with hyperendemic malaria transmission. *($5,475,000)*
2. Logistic assistance will be provided by PMI to transport the procured nets from the central level to select provinces. *($2,175,000)*
3. PMI will support routine distribution of nets through ANC for pregnant women and EPI for children under five and possibly additional channels, if appropriate. *($1,885,000)*
4. Technical assistance will help in-country stakeholders implement continuous distribution strategy (developed with FY 2015 funds) to improve ITN coverage in high burden provinces *($270,000)*

2. Vector Control

NMCP/PMI objectives
The MoH in the revised National Malaria Strategic Plan 2016-2020 plans to reduce malaria mortality by 60% from the 2012 data using proven interventions, such as indoor residual spraying (IRS). The Plan's objective for IRS is that by the end of 2020, at least 60% of homes in at-risk municipalities have been sprayed. The IRS coverage has been reduced, however, to the border areas with Namibia and Zambia. PMI has supported IRS in Angola with procurement, implementation, and technical assistance between 2005 and 2014. PMI has transitioned out of implementation support for IRS; the MoH has not prioritized IRS at the national level and shifted the responsibility of IRS to the provinces and municipalities, where there has been interest, but not yet financial commitment.

Progress since PMI was launched
PMI first implemented IRS with the WHO in Cunene and Huila Provinces in 2005. Namibe Province was added in 2006 but by 2008, both Namibe and Cunene were dropped and Huambo Province (previously a province with high transmission) was added. In 2010, Cunene was again added at the request of the NMCP, in support of Namibia's malaria pre-elimination efforts and as part of the Southern African Development Community plans for the elimination of malaria in

the region. IRS was focused in municipalities where there is greatest movement between Angola and Namibia. Since 2005 pyrethroids have been used in all spray campaigns, based on susceptibility testing.

Table 4 shows a list of PMI-supported IRS activities during 2010-2014, including coverage and areas where IRS was used. In these areas where IRS has been used, PMI has tested for insecticide susceptibility annually. PMI used the WHO cone bioassay tests to determine quality of spraying activities and decay rates. Since there is not a susceptible colony of *Anopheles* mosquitoes in Angola, WHO cone bioassays have been conducted with mosquitoes collected as larvae from the field, reared to adults and then used for the testing. This method of conducting cone bioassays is not ideal, as confounding factors such as insecticide resistance may make it difficult to interpret the cone bioassay data. This was shown in 2013, when mortality dropped to under 50% at three months post-spraying with deltamethrin in Bailundo municipality. Cone assays immediately after spraying indicated that the quality of spray was adequate. Testing of insecticide potency at CDC confirmed that the quality of insecticide met the required specification. However, insecticide resistance testing using the CDC Bottle Assay confirmed low levels of insecticide resistance to deltamethrin.

For the monitoring of IRS and ITN programs, a colony of insecticide susceptible mosquitoes is required. There is currently no susceptible colony of mosquitoes in Angola and this is affecting the ability to monitor the residual effects of IRS and ITN programs. PMI supported the construction of an entomology laboratory/insectary in 2014 to support IRS entomologic monitoring and evaluation in Huambo, and to serve as the first insectary in Angola since the end of the civil war. The entomology laboratory can support the rearing of mosquitoes and perform basic entomologic activities such as mosquito morphological identification and sample processing. The insectary can be used to rear a susceptible laboratory colony of *Anopheles* mosquitoes. The insectary was constructed from a large container and is located on the grounds of the Huambo Provincial Hospital.

Due to lack of entomologists and entomology technicians in Angola, PMI has supported a number of entomology trainings focused on field mosquito collection techniques, mosquito identification, mosquito rearing techniques, and insecticide resistance testing using the WHO susceptibility tests and the CDC Bottle Assay. Trainings, conducted with the NMCP, have included personnel from selected provincial and district health authorities and in some instances with personnel from other institutes such as the *Instituto de Investigação Agronomica* in Huambo.

Table 4: PMI-supported IRS activities 2010 - 2014

Calendar Year	Name of Provinces Sprayed*	Insecticide Used	Number of Structures Sprayed	Coverage Rate	Population Protected
2010	Huambo, Huila, Cunene	Lamdacyhalothrin	135,856	96%	649,842
2011	Huambo, Huila, Cunene	Deltamethrin	145,264	98%	689,668
2012	Huambo, Huila, Cunene	Deltamethrin	141,782	97.7%	676,090
2013	Huambo, Huila, Cunene	Deltamethrin	98,136	92.1%	419,353
2014**	Huambo (Bailundo Municipality only)	Deltamethrin	14,649	88.7%	58,370

* In each province, only selected municipalities have been sprayed, thus the whole province has not received IRS.
** 2014 was the final year PMI supported implementation of IRS in Angola.

Progress during the last 12-18 months

During 2014, PMI supported the final year of IRS implementation. The spray campaign was conducted October 1 – November 8, 2014 in one municipality in Huambo province (see Table 4, above). WHO cone bioassay testing was done in five sentinel villages in Bailundo Municipality to evaluate the quality of spraying. The quality assurance was done within the first two weeks of spraying where ten houses were tested in each sentinel village using field-collected larvae and pupae reared to adults in the insectary. Testing results demonstrated some low mortality in houses tested in Sachole and Velha Chica villages, while other sentinel site mortality was high. Therefore, the PMI implementing partner conducted a spray technique refresher training immediately over two consecutive days to all spray operators, team leaders and supervisors to ensure delivery of quality spraying and better supervision. While the PMI implementing partner planned to re-test these two villages soon thereafter, the larvae scarcity precluded the retesting from taking place.

Bioassays were also repeated in monthly intervals at the same sentinel sites to monitor residual efficacy/decay rates of the insecticides. It was observed that 24-hour mortality rates were markedly lower during December 2014 and January 2015 in all sites. In these bioassay tests wild caught *Anopheles* species were used, assuming that they were *An. gambiae s.l*. However, for all tests it was noted that most of the mosquitoes were not *An. gambiae s.l*, but *An. rufipes, An. coustani, An. maculipalplis, An. longipalpis, An. squamosus, An. marshalli, An. theileri* and very few *An. funestus*. Most of them were *An. rufipes* and *An. coustani*; this was confirmed from the specimens sent to the Centers for Disease Control, Atlanta and Wits Research Institute for Malaria in South Africa University. Hence, it was also decided to conduct some refresher training for entomological staff on morphological identification.

Subsequently, PMI has shifted its focus to provide technical assistance to those provinces or municipalities interested in assuming financial responsibility for undertaking IRS. For example, the provinces of Benguela, Cunene, and Huila have demonstrated strong interest. PMI supported a workshop in April 2015 to educate representatives of selected DPS about IRS – the benefits, the process, and the budget required. While there was interest, at the time of writing, no commitment to establish an IRS program had been formalized

Entomological Surveillance

In 2014, PMI supported insecticide resistance monitoring in Bailundo Municipality (Huambo Province), where IRS was to be conducted in 2014. The results indicated that there was no resistance in *An.gambiae s.l.* to deltamethrin (a pyrethroid), bendiocarb (a carbamate), or fenitrothion (an organophosphate).

PMI continues to conduct longitudinal entomologic surveillance in former IRS areas, for vector species, abundance, resting behavior, and mosquito malaria infection rates in Huambo and Huila at total of six sentinel sites. Since May 2014, there were four sentinel sites in Huambo Province spread between the three municipalities of Huambo (former IRS area), Caala (non-IRS area) and Bailundo (2014 IRS area). In Huila, there were two sentinel sites in the municipality of Chiba one in a former IRS area and the other in a non-IRS area. Monthly mosquito collections were from CDC light traps, pyrethrum spray collections, and pit traps. In Huila, the number of *Anopheles* collected were low in both sites, ranging from 0 – 1.5 mosquitoes/house/day. In Huambo, the highest collections were from the Bailundo municipality ranging from 0 – 11.4 mosquitoes/house per day, with the highest collections in May and June. Initial analysis by morphological identification of these mosquitoes was conducted at Witwatersrand University, South Africa. However, since this institute have not been able to perform molecular analysis on mosquitoes that are not from the *An. gambiae* and *An, funestus* complex, these samples will be sent to elsewhere for species identification by molecular analysis.

In consultation with the NMCP, PMI has helped to create provincial teams to build capacity to undertake basic entomology work and engage directly with provincial health directors at the Provincial Health Departments (DPS). Once provincial governors decide to participate, a memorandum of understanding with individual provinces to clarify roles and responsibilities will be established. PMI supported the NMCP interest in conducting national insecticide resistance studies aimed at establishment of provincial capacity to carry out insecticide resistance monitoring and determining of vector resistance in Angola to insecticides currently being deployed. In December 2014, PMI conducted a training for provincial and municipal health authorities for insecticide resistance testing in Zaire, Uige, Malanje, Luanda, Namibe, Huambo, Cunene, Benguela, and Huila. These nine provinces represent the malaria stratification of the three endemic areas of the country. In January 2015, PMI supported a study to evaluate vector insecticide resistance. Preliminary results of this evaluation show that malaria vectors in Angola are starting to develop resistance to pyrethroids, deltamethrin, and lambda-cyhalothrin. This evaluation also showed very high or 100% susceptibility of malaria vectors to bendiocarb and pirimiphos-methyl. The mosquitoes from this evaluation will be identified by molecular assays at the CDC.

In 2014, PMI supported species identification of 260 mosquitoes, mainly from insecticide resistance testing. Of those, only 11.5% was *An. gambiae s.s.*. The majority of the mosquitoes were *An. rufipes* (61.9%) and *An. coustani* (21.8%). Low numbers of *An. maculipalplis* (1.5%) and *An. longipalpis* (0.3%) were found. A sample of 45 mosquitoes, from the longitudinal monitoring, analyzed by Witwatersrand University were 33% *An. funestus s.s*, 11% *An. gambiae s.s* and 2% *An. arabiensis*. *An. rufupes* (15.5%) and *An. squamosus* (15.5%) were the other two most predominant species of mosquitoes collected. Other species identified included *An. vandeeni*, *An. marshallii* and *An. ziemanni*. These may be non-vectors, secondary vectors, or become the main vectors during certain times of the year. Additional information, such as feeding habits, human-bite rates, host preferences, resting habits, and sporozoite infection rates are necessary to determine vectorial capacity of these mosquitoes and their role in malaria transmission in Angola.

Plans and justification
PMI will no longer provide support for implementation of IRS activities, but will continue to support entomologic and epidemiologic monitoring in order to determine the effects of IRS withdrawal on the entomologic and epidemiologic setting. This technical assistance is needed due to the minimal entomologic capacity in country and the need to continue to understand how malaria transmission is occurring in Angola and post-IRS settings. There will be continued trainings to improve mosquito identification skills, build local provincial and district capacity to perform mosquito collections, insecticide resistance tests and longitudinal entomological surveillance. Training in mosquito rearing techniques will be focused at sites where mosquito rearing will take place. The technical assistance will include species identification, susceptibility studies and vector density monitoring. Monitoring in Malanje, Huambo, and Cunene will continue monthly at one to two sites per province. In addition to this technical support, PMI will continue to advocate at the national and provincial levels for the GRA to be more engaged and take greater ownership of its entomological monitoring, including salaries and materials for Angolan entomologists and management of the insectary. Technical assistance trips by CDC entomologists will occur to strengthen and oversee the activities that are done in a field setting. PMI will continue to support molecular analysis support for mosquito identification while it continues to work with the MoH to build up their PCR capacity within the country. PMI will also provide the needed supplies and reagents such as field collecting material, entomologic supplies to support Huambo entomology laboratory and insectary, insecticide resistance testing material to perform these entomologic activities.

Proposed activities with FY 2016 funding: ($750,000)
1. PMI will strategically shift from providing IRS support and technical assistance to developing a greater knowledge of the entomologic map in Angola through entomologic surveillance in select provinces. Entomologic surveillance will include species identification, susceptibility studies, and vector density monitoring. PMI will develop capacity at both the central and provincial levels and work in areas where IRS

susceptibility studies were undertaken, as well as in Lunda Norte and Lunda Sul. Specifically, entomologic monitoring will occur in in three malaria transmission zones, and in provinces where PMI has previously supported IRS, as well as two new provinces. Furthermore, all areas evaluated will have received ITNs during the mass campaign. Proposed area for entomologic monitoring are: Cunene Province, an epidemic transmission zone and border province with Namibia; Huambo Province, in a mesoendemic transmission zone which currently has low malaria prevalence; Malange Province, a high transmission zone where there has been no IRS but has relatively high net coverage; Lunda Norte Province, a high transmission zone that received Global Fund nets in 2014; and Lunda Sul Province, site of a recently completed therapeutic efficacy survey (TES) that received Global Fund nets in 2014. PMI will continue to advocate at the provincial level for funding for entomological activities and staff, and to emphasize the critical importance of entomological capacity to monitor vector control efforts. *($650,000)*

2. Currently there is no molecular laboratory in Angola where mosquitoes from entomologic surveillance from either the PMI or the NMCP program can be analyzed. To date, mosquitoes have been outsourced for analysis. In 2014, an NMCP Laboratory Advisor underwent a month-long training at the CDC on malaria molecular diagnostic techniques. In 2015, PMI will be supporting a feasibility assessment for building in-country capacity and establishing a molecular laboratory in Angola. With FY 2016 funds, PMI will continue to support PCR activities will while capacity is developed and maintained in Angola. PMI will continue to provide molecular analysis using PCR techniques to identify and confirm mosquito species. *($60,000)*

3. For continued support, CDC will provide two technical assistance trips to maintain strides made in entomologic monitoring and insecticide resistance testing at the central level. The support also includes reagents for entomologic testing and other laboratory diagnostic equipment and supplies. *($40,000)*

3. Malaria in pregnancy

NMCP/PMI objectives
The NMCP has a three-pronged approach to malaria prevention and control during pregnancy, including IPTp, ITN use, and diagnosis and treatment of clinical illness in line with WHO recommendations. According to its strategic plan, the NMCP has the following objectives for malaria in pregnancy (MIP):

- By the end of 2020, at least 80% of pregnant women sleep under an ITN.
- By the end of 2020, 80% of pregnant women have access to prenatal consultations and those eligible for IPTp receive at least three doses of SP.
- By the end of 2020, at least 80% of all patients with malaria receive diagnosis and treatment conforming to national standards at all levels of the health system.

Progress since PMI was launched
The 2011 MIS revealed that only 17.5% of pregnant women declared having taken at least two doses of IPTp during their last pregnancy. In 2013, in accordance with the new WHO guidelines, the NMCP adopted the new IPTp policy that IPTp be given to all pregnant women in areas of

moderate to high malaria transmission at each scheduled ANC visit, except during the first trimester. Each SP dose should be given at least one month apart and the last dose can be administered up to the time of delivery, without safety concerns. A pregnant woman should not receive folic acid at a daily dose equal to or greater than 5 mg along with SP, because it counteracts SP's efficacy as an antimalarial. Thus, the recommended daily dose of folic acid is 0.4 mg. While the recommended dosage is now listed in the new essential drugs list, the revised list is still awaiting approval by the Ministry of Health. Once the list is approved, the recommended dose should be procured for Angola, however the dosage of folic acid currently available in Angola is still 5 mg. This policy currently applies to the entire country, including epidemic-prone areas in the south. Data from the reproductive health department's routine information system states that the policy is being implemented in all units with prenatal appointments in operation.

However, most health centers do not provide ANC services and do not provide IPTp. According to IBEP 2008/9, less than half of pregnant women attend four or more antenatal visits, and only 42% of births occur in a health facility, due to this limited access. That said, if access to ANC services improved, IPTp rates would increase. The 2014 NMCP data indicate that of 916,533 pregnant women who made their first prenatal care visit, 63% received the first dose of IPTp, 48% the second dose, and 6% the third dose. The low ANC coverage in Angola may be related to social and cultural factors, and not merely a result of the lack of health centers providing ANC services. One potential channel for increasing IPTp use could be via the ADECOS at the community level.

Since 2012, there have been many stockouts of ITNs for routine distribution through ANC due to numerous delays in procuring the ITNs needed for continuous distribution. Furthermore, since 2013, the NMCP has shifted all resources to support the mass distribution campaign, with ITNs that had been planned for routine distribution via ANC reallocated to the campaign. However, upon completion of the campaign, nets procured for routine distribution will be used for ANC and EPI. As for stockouts of SP, the NMCP plans to address this through a new policy of distributing SP only to health facilities providing ANC services.

With regard to the treatment of uncomplicated malaria in pregnancy, NMCP policy is to administer oral quinine during the first semester and ACTs during the two last semesters of the pregnancy. For severe malaria, the first-line treatment is artesunate IV, with artemether IM as second line, and quinine IV as the third line. However, since artesunate and artemether are often not available, quinine is the treatment most often administered.

Progress during the last 12- 18 months
PMI collaborated with the NMCP, the Reproductive Health and the HIV departments to update the *National Protocol for Malaria in Pregnancy*. As of July 2015, approval of the MoH for reproduction and dissemination of the manual was pending.

PMI continued to support partners in nine provinces to improve access to malaria prevention and treatment services for pregnant women. PMI continues to support trainings of health workers on prevention and treatment of malaria in pregnancy (see table below).

Table 5. Health workers trained in malaria in pregnancy (FY 2014) and future targets

Provinces	# Facilities providing ANC	ANC 1 attendance rate	# ANC Health Workers	# ANC Health Workers Trained	# ANC Health Workers to be trained by the end of FY 2015	Remaining # to be trained in FY 2016
C. Norte	27	22%	**81**	20	25	36
C. Sul	121	48%	**363**	181	22	160
Huambo*	200	86%	**600**	0	0	600
Benguela	143	60%	**429**	303	126	0
Zaire	57	55%	**171**	33	0	138
Malange	32	21%	**96**	96	0	0
Uige	51	15%	**153**	84	36	33
Huila	166	60%	**498**	246	54	198
Luanda*	164	75%	**293**	224	69	TBD
Total	**961**		**2,684**	**1,187**	**332**	**1,165**

*PMI's implementing partner who has been working in Huambo and Luanda conducted integrated trainings on malaria prevention and treatment, which includes MIP. PMI has phased out of Huambo; in FY 2014, 293 health workers were trained in Luanda.

In 2014, PMI's implementing partner found that IPTp coverage increased significantly in Angola, from 2% in 2006/7 to 18% in 2011. This increase was also shown by the NMCP routine HMIS data, where the numbers of pregnant women who attended ANC and received IPTp almost doubled between 2007 and 2011. This trend is as expected since IPTp was introduced in Angola in 2006 and implementation was scaled up thereafter.

The GRA continues to reaffirm its commitment to procure IPTp for SP. Based on discussions with NMCP, PMI anticipates that the GRA will be able to procure sufficient amounts and PMI will continue to work with all levels of the supply chain to ensure that there are not stockouts at health facility level. Since PMI does not procure SP in Angola, a SP commodity gap analysis table has not been included.

Plans and justification
PMI will continue to sustain and build on increasing IPTp rates for the upcoming year. PMI will support the health facilities to continue to strengthen ANC services, maintain support for training and supervision, print revised training manuals, and promote early and regular ANC attendance.

Proposed activities with FY 2016 funding: ($400,000)
PMI will continue to collaborate with the NMCP and Reproductive Health Division to strengthen prevention, diagnosis, and treatment of malaria in pregnancy at different levels: municipal and health facility levels and at the community level. The proposed activities are cross cutting with some ITN activities, case management, and BCC activities.

1. Training and supervision of healthcare workers in select provinces (see Table 5 for FY 2016 targets), and dissemination of current policy to provide at least three doses of SP at the municipal and facility levels. *($100,000)*
2. IEC/BCC for malaria in pregnancy at the community level: Develop BCC strategy with appropriate, targeted messages for the community, focusing in particular on rural population with low education. This will include developing and conducting training for outreach workers, improving communication skills, producing materials for distribution to incentivize IPTp and ITN use by identifying and promoting positive behavior. *($100,000)*
3. Strengthen malaria in pregnancy services at health facilities: Training and regular supervisions of healthcare providers will improve the diagnosis and treatment of malaria in pregnant women. *($200,000)*
4. Support routine ITN distribution through ANC (further description and costs covered under the ITN section).

4. Case management

a. Diagnosis and Treatment

NMCP/PMI objectives
PMI is working to help the NMCP to achieve its objective that by 2020, 100% of all suspect cases at health facilities and in the community will be tested for malaria prior to treatment. The NMCP is committed to the expansion of access to ACTs, with the objective that 100% of all malaria cases seen in health facilities and the community be treated in accordance with national treatment guidelines by 2020.

Progress since PMI was launched
PMI has supported the NMCP as the country has transitioned from routine clinical diagnosis of malaria to laboratory confirmation of all suspect malaria cases. Since 2006, PMI has procured and delivered to all provinces over 10 million RDTs and over 260 microscopes and malaria microscopy kits.

PMI and its partners have invested in training of laboratory technicians in malaria diagnosis, including the training of 6,275 health workers in diagnosis since 2006. In addition, since 2006, PMI has supported the training and mentorship of 11 national level laboratory trainers and supervisors that make up the lead team to train and supervise the provinces. PMI continues to support training of laboratory staff in nine provinces through NGOs (reaching eight provinces through the PMI-supported NGO strengthening project and a ninth through the USAID integrated health systems strengthening project).

PMI has been supporting the expansion of access to ACTs since its beginning in Angola. Since 2006, PMI has procured nearly 25 million ACTs in Angola and trained nearly 16,000 healthcare workers in ACT use.

In light of relatively low levels of access to the public health sector, PMI supported a pilot project to provide malaria testing and treatment through private pharmacies in Huambo Province. In 2008, PMI assisted the NMCP to implement a pilot project in selected municipalities in Huambo Province to improve accessibility and effective use of ACTs in pharmacies through subsidized sales of Coartem®. This project was launched in July 2009 and since then Coartem® has been sold at private pharmacies registered by the Huambo DPS.

PMI has supported two therapeutic efficacy studies (TES) in Angola. Another GRA 2004 study found a high (100%) rate of efficacy of both AL and AS-AQ in Huambo Province. A 2013 TES conducted in Uige and Zaire Provinces found PCR-corrected efficacy of DP of 100% in both Uige and Zaire, and a PCR-corrected efficacy of AL of 97% in Uige and 88% in Zaire. Although there was molecular evidence of lumefantrine resistance in Zaire Province, all of the treatment failures were wildtype for the K13 artemisinin resistance marker. In 2015, a TES of all three drugs is being conducted in Benguela, Lunda Sul, and Zaire Provinces.

Progress during the last 12-18 months
PMI procured and distributed 2.8 million RDTs in FY 2014. During this period, PMI and its partners supported the training of 1,092 health workers in malaria diagnostics, focused primarily on eight selected target provinces. PMI also procured and distributed 720,390 ACTs during FY 2014, and trained over 3,000 healthcare workers in ACT use, with trainings primarily conducted in the target provinces (with a total of 13,116 health workers). PMI and its partners have continued to provide supervision to health facilities in target provinces, which include assessment of diagnosis and case management knowledge and practices by healthcare workers and laboratory technicians. Challenges encountered in Angola include low access of the population to the public health sector, a low proportion of health facilities providing microscopy services, stockouts of ACTs and RDTs, poor capacity of healthcare workers and laboratory technicians, and failure of healthcare workers to interpret test results to correctly prescribe treatment. Although data reported through the parallel NMCP reporting and recording system indicate that 85% of suspect cases were tested either by RDT or microscopy in 2014, these data likely significantly overestimate the true testing rate.

The pilot project providing sales of subsided ACTs in Huambo Province was expanded to include administration of RDTs at 50 private pharmacies participating in the project in Huambo. The PMI partner and NMCP were able to successfully negotiate with provincial authorities to allow select private pharmacies to test for malaria using RDT, an obstacle in previous years. In the new model, private pharmacies buy ACTs and RDTs from the PMI partner, and then sell a malaria test and treatment "service." Patients pay a small fee and are administered an RDT, and if positive, receive an ACT. The pilot project is currently being expanded to 33 pharmacies in Uíge Province. The project is expected to transition to be self-sustaining by FY 2016 [see Pharmaceutical Management Section].

Commodity gap analysis

The following tables summarize the result of the gap analyses for RDTs and ACTs in Angola. Given the uncertainty of Global Fund support in Angola, any potential Global Fund contribution of RDTs and ACTs was not included in the gap analyses.

Table 6: RDT Gap Analysis

Calendar Year	2015	2016	2017
RDT Needs			
Target population at risk for malaria	25,041,650	25,717,775	26,412,155
Total number projected fever cases seeking care in the public sector[a]	8,037,769	9,114,662	9,890,612
Percent of fever cases confirmed with microscopy[b]	30%	35%	40%
Percent of fever cases confirmed with RDT	70%	65%	60%
Fever cases tested by RDT in the private sector	0	198,780	165,000
Total RDT Needs	**5,626,438**	**6,123,310**	**6,099,367**
Partner Contributions			
RDTs carried over (deficit) from previous year	0	0	0
RDTs from MoH[c]	1,500,000	1,600,000	0
RDTs from Global Fund	0	0	0
RDTs from other donors	0	0	0
RDTs planned with PMI funding	2,500,000	1,700,000	5,800,000
Total RDTs Available	**4,000,000**	**3,300,000**	**5,800,000**
Total RDT Surplus (Gap)	**(1,626,438)**	**(2,823,310)**	**(299,367)**

[a] Total number of fever cases expected at public health facilities, assuming 1.50 fever cases in children <3, 1 fever case in children 3-8, 0.63 fever cases in children 9-14 and 0.38 fever cases in children >14 and adults per year, and adjusting for the proportion of the population with access to the public sector. The true number of fever cases is likely higher than the projected numbers, but the figures in the table reflect observed health-seeking behavior in Angola, and are consistent with the number of febrile episodes reported by health facilities.

[b] Currently, only a small subset of health facilities in Angola have sufficient laboratory capacity to perform microscopy for malaria. However, as the GRA continues to expand the number of health facilities and enhance lab capacity at existing health facilities, laboratory capacity is expected to improve over the next few years. As a result, NMCP expects microscopy to have an increasing share of all malaria diagnostic tests.

[c] Given the current financial crisis in Angola and lack of movement on MoH procurements to date, it is unlikely that these contributions will be forthcoming. Thus, the RDT gap will most likely be even higher than estimated.

Table 7: ACT Gap Analysis

Calendar Year	2015	2016	2017
ACT Needs			
Target population at risk for malaria	25,041,650	25,717,775	26,412,155
Total projected number of malaria cases seeking care in the public sector[a]	2,900,406	2,968,737	2,996,945
Malaria cases treated with ACTs in the private sector	0	174,540	144,300
Total ACT Needs	**2,900,406**	**3,143,277**	**3,141,245**
Partner Contributions			
ACTs carried over (deficit) from previous year	0	0	56,723
ACTs from MoH[b]	1,100,000	1,200,000	0
ACTs from Global Fund	0	0	0
ACTs from other donors	0	0	0
ACTs planned with PMI funding	1,366,950	2,000,000	3,300,000
Total ACTs Available	**2,466,950**	**3,200,000**	**3,356,723**
Total ACT Surplus (Gap)	**(433,456)**	**56,723**	**215,478**

[a] Calculated on the basis of the number of tested fever cases (see RDT gap analysis) and assuming a test positivity rate of 36.6% in 2015, 33.0% in 2016, and 30.7% in 2017, and assuming that 94% of malaria cases will be uncomplicated

[b] Given the current financial crisis in Angola and lack of movement on MoH procurements to date, it is unlikely that these contributions will be forthcoming. Thus, the ACT gap will most likely be higher than estimated.

Plans and justification
Given uncertainties in Global Fund and GRA funding for malaria commodities, and recent nationwide stockouts of malaria commodities, NMCP has requested continued PMI support for malaria commodities procurement, including laboratory diagnostic reagents and supplies not available locally in Angola, RDTs, ACTs, and treatments for severe malaria. (Traditionally, the

GRA has been responsible for procurement of severe malaria treatments; however, the NMCP has requested PMI support this year.) PMI will procure RDTs and ACTs at a ratio of approximately 2.35 to 1, derived from a reported test positivity rate of 43% nationwide in 2014. In line with PMI policy, the RDTs will be single-species *Plasmodium falciparum* tests. Following NMCP strategy to preferentially use AS-AQ in the pediatric population, PMI will procure AS-AQ and prioritize infant and young child formulations. In accordance with NMCP strategy that 30% of severe malaria cases be treated with injectable artesunate and 70% with intramuscular artemether, PMI will procure 30,000 treatments of injectable artesunate, and 70,000 treatments of intramuscular artemether, representing roughly 55% of total demand for severe malaria treatments (estimated to be 182,185 in 2017[4]). It is planned to use intramuscular artemether preferentially in peripheral health facilities, while reserving injectable artesunate for larger hospitals with the capacity to provide IV treatment. While the GRA remains responsible for the procurement of severe malaria supplies, PMI plans to procure a limited amount of intramuscular artemether to complement the GRA's continued efforts to procure quality-assured parenteral artemisinin derivatives.

Within the context of nationwide stockouts resulting from the Ministry of Health not procuring the commodities it had been expected to, the end of the Global Fund grant, and the inability of PMI alone to fill the enormous gap for ACTs and RDTs, PMI has decided to direct the commodities it procures to be distributed in the highest malaria burden provinces, instead of across all 18 provinces. PMI recognizes that all Angolans deserve access to life-saving commodities. However, in the current context PMI must prioritize the most vulnerable people living in the high-risk areas where PMI hopes to make the most impact in reducing malaria morbidity and mortality. PMI will continue to encourage Angolan government leadership at the national and provincial levels to increase its commitment to malaria control.

Since expansion of access to RDTs and ACTs necessarily involves improving case management at the health facility level, PMI will continue to support training and supervision of healthcare workers and laboratory technicians. Capitalizing on the presence of provincial and municipal malaria supervisors, PMI will work to strengthen their capacity to train and supervise healthcare workers on malaria case management. This will involve training the supervisors on formative supervision and supporting them to be able to conduct regular, scheduled supervisions in health facilities in their areas. Similarly, PMI will support and train provincial-level laboratory supervisors to build their technical capacity to properly conduct trainings and formative supervisions, and provide them logistical support to conduct regular, scheduled supervisions in laboratories in their areas. These activities will be focused in priority provinces, comprising the northern, hyperendemic provinces.

The NMCP, with PMI support, is advocating that the upcoming community health worker program (ADECOS) eventually include malaria diagnosis and treatment as part of integrated community case management of childhood illness. As currently planned, the activities of the first round of ADECOS to be trained will be restricted to community mobilization, but PMI supports NMCP's strategy to implement a pilot test of iCCM in ADECOS as a first step to expanding the

---

[4] Assuming 6% of all malaria cases seen at public health facilities will be severe.

community health worker program to include malaria case management. Thus, PMI will continue to support piloting an iCCM program that could be expanded to all CHWs (an iCCM in Uige Province is planned with FY 2015 funds). Data collected from this pilot program are expected to allow NMCP to advocate for the policy that all community health workers perform malaria diagnosis and treatment in their communities.

Proposed activities with FY 2016 funding: ($9,295,000)

1. *Procurement of laboratory supplies for malaria diagnosis:* Procurement of laboratory diagnostic reagents and supplies not available locally in Angola *($50,000)*
2. *Procurement of RDTs:* Procurement of approximately 5,800,000 RDTs for the public sector and private sector *($3,120,000)*
3. *Procurement of ACTs:* Procurement of approximately 3,300,000 treatments of ASAQ for the public sector *($2,065,000)*
4. *Procurement of injectable artesunate for treatment of severe malaria:* Procurement of approximately 30,000 treatments[5] of injectable artesunate for treatment of severe malaria *($60,000)*
5. *Procurement of intramuscular artemether for treatment of severe malaria:* Procurement of approximately 70,000 treatments of intramuscular artemether for treatment of severe malaria *($140,000)*
6. *Strengthen malaria case management:* Training and supporting formative supervision for provincial and health facility health workers to improve malaria case management. This activity will also include: (1) Training of trainers at the provincial and municipal level of malaria supervisors on conducting formative supervision; and (2) support to municipal level (malaria supervisors) to provide regular supervision visits to health facilities on a quarterly basis. All trainings will be coordinated with NMCP. The geographic focus will be the highly endemic areas in the north and east of the country, including provinces previously not covered by PMI support. *($3,000,000)*
7. *Training and supervision on laboratory diagnosis (microscopy) and quality control:* Training and supporting formative supervision for provincial and municipal laboratory supervisors to improve malaria diagnostics in the laboratory, training of trainers at the provincial of laboratory supervisors on conducting formative supervision *($600,000)*
8. *Expand support to iCCM/ADECOS activity:* Continue to support the GRA's iCCM initiative with ADECOS (community health workers) in select municipalities. PMI will provide RDTs and ACTs; the MoH will provide commodities for the other diseases included in the care package (ex. pneumonia, diarrhea) *($200,000)*
9. *Technical assistance to support continuation and sustainable transition of private sector case management services activity:* Prepare for potential Global Fund support for expansion of private sector case management services pilot *($60,000)*

---

[5] Cost of treatment with either injectable artesunate or intramuscular artemether was estimated to be $2 per severe malaria treatment, calculated based on the assumption that 75% of severe malaria cases will occur in children <5

b. Pharmaceutical Management

Pharmaceutical products entering Angola are supposed to be registered through the National Directorate of Medicines and Equipment (DNME) before entry and distribution. The Department of Pharmaceutical Inspection within the MoH conducts border and post-marketing inspections. At present, all products that need to be tested are sent to laboratories in Portugal or Brazil as there is no in-country capacity for in-depth quality assurance testing. The DNME also has a Department of Pharmacovigilance established to track adverse events from medications. A PMI and USAID-supported assessment of the medicines regulatory system and supply chain identified several key concerns, including an insufficient legal framework, limited human resource capacity, and an inadequate quality control system.

Products purchased by the GRA are stored and managed at the parastatal central medical stores (Central Unit for Procurement and Provision of Medicines and Medical Supplies [CECOMA]). Since 2009, PMI has supported an augmented supply chain system for PMI-procured commodities; all commodities are delivered directly to the provincial warehouses, bypassing CECOMA. The provinces then assume responsibility for the ultimate delivery to health facility level. Delivery from provinces to health facilities remains weak, with some provincial warehouses with expiring stocks while health facilities have stockouts. At the national level, proper quantification and forecasting of malaria commodities have been challenged by a lack of consumption data and a weak logistics management information system.

As in many other parts of sub-Saharan Africa and Southeast Asia, drug quality is also a significant concern in Angola. In late 2012, the DNME seized a large shipment of counterfeit ACTs at the port in Luanda. It alerted all public facilities and private pharmacies that an additional shipment had infiltrated the market and took measures to confiscate these products. The GRA does not yet have a qualified central level laboratory or an adequate surveillance system to systematically evaluate the quality of pharmaceutical commodities coming into Angola.

NMCP/PMI objectives
PMI and the NMCP's goals are to prevent stockouts of ACTs, RDTs, severe malaria treatments, and other malaria-related commodities at public health facilities. PMI is committed to working with DNME and CECOMA to strengthen the GRA national distribution system to the point that it can assume distribution of government- and donor-supplied malaria commodities.

Progress since PMI was launched
The process of delivering PMI-procured commodities directly to the provincial warehouses has proven to be efficient. PMI-procured supplies are usually delivered to all provincial warehouses within two weeks of arrival in the country. PMI recognizes the need to engage in capacity building and the development of sustainable systems and therefore has supported supply chain strengthening through multiple channels: the USAID integrated supply chain strengthening project; the USAID integrated health systems strengthening project that works with municipalities in Huambo and Luanda Provinces for budgeting, planning and M&E; and the NGO strengthening project in eight provinces that supported activities at the health facility level.

40

In late 2012, PMI assisted the NMCP to quantify and forecast malaria commodity needs for 2013 through 2015. In order to build capacity for the NMCP to conduct quantification routinely and independently, a five-day workshop was conducted to strengthen the understanding of quantification methods and develop terms of reference for the national quantification technical working group.

PMI has supported an integrated USAID supply chain system strengthening project which has been working closely with CECOMA to develop an operational strategy, standard operating procedures, terms of reference for staff, tools for storage and distribution, performance indicators, tools for operations management, and a logistic management information system. At lower levels, PMI-supported partners have supported improved stock management at the provincial and health facility level. This includes training on stock management, provision of tools and job aids, and supervision. All training and supervision tools used are uniform and approved by the MoH.

Progress during the last 12-18 months
PMI, through the integrated USAID supply chain system strengthening project, continued to work with CECOMA, DNME, and the Inspector General for Health to build their institutional capacity, improve warehouse management processes and procedures, and to strengthen pharmaceutical regulatory functions. With PMI support, both entities developed annual work plans with budgets, with the goal of leading to a comprehensive national supply chain strategy. Concurrently, PMI provided assistance to the NMCP in the data-driven development of quarterly distribution plans to efficiently distribute malaria commodities to the provinces, as well as a forecasting tool to predict future demand for malaria commodities.

PMI's implementing partner has been building the institutional capacity of CECOMA through the review of key standard operating procedures for receiving, inventory management, dispatch and distribution; the development of human resource capacity and performance improvement indicators; and performance monitoring and metrics. For example, according to established Key Performance Indicators and benchmarks, there has been improvements in tracking of delivery notes from 56% to 96%, order accuracy from 94% to 100%, and dispatch timeliness (99.5%). CECOMA has demonstrated improvement through its successful distribution of Global Fund commodities as well as GRA-procured antimalarial commodities.

At the provincial level, PMI, through the integrated USAID supply chain system strengthening project, supported capacity building in pharmaceutical management of municipal teams in Luanda, Huambo, Bié, Cunene, Huila and Uíge. In addition, the PMI NGO-strengthening project has continued to provide strengthen capacity at the health facility level.

PMI supported EUV surveys in June 2014 and December 2014. The most recent survey, which included 42 health facilities in 5 provinces, found high rates of 50% ACT and RDT stockouts on the day of visit, and widespread weaknesses in commodities management, including the lack of use of stock cards.

Plans and justification
PMI will continue to strengthen Ministry of Health in pharmaceutical management. PMI will provide technical assistance to the DNME, the Inspectorate General, and the NMCP in all steps of the procurement and distribution process: quantifying and forecasting demand of malaria commodities; procurement of quality malaria commodities; testing and quality assurance/quality control QA/QC of malaria commodities; planning distributions in accordance with needs; and distributing in an efficient and timely manner. Assistance will have an emphasis on sustainability and capacity building, creating the appropriate regulatory framework and training a skilled cadre to continue to strengthen the Ministry of Health distribution system. While the eventual transition to a single distribution system is prepared, PMI will continue to support a separate distribution system for PMI-procured commodities from port to the provincial level.

In addition, PMI will provide technical assistance as the private sector RDT and ACT pilot project expands and transitions to be self-sustainable. Following negotiations with NMCP and Global Fund, Global Fund is expected to assume support for the expansion of the private sector case management activity. PMI will provide technical assistance to aid in the expansion of the project in FY 2016.

Proposed activities with FY 2016 funding: ($1,350,000)

1. *Technical assistance and support for import, clearance, storage, distribution and management of RDT and ACT commodities:* Provide assistance in the distribution from port, and storage through customs, and down through provincial level of PMI-procured RDT and ACT commodities. *($300,000)*
2. *Strengthen Ministry of Health antimalarial drug management system*: Strengthen pharmaceutical management related to antimalarial drugs including regular supervision, provincial training of pharmacist, help with printing of supply chain management forms. Strengthen capacity at NMCP to forecast demand and distribute commodities in line with prioritized needs. *($650,000)*
3. *Strengthen Ministry of Health QA/QC systems and capacity*: Quality of GRA-procured ACTs and RDTs remain a major constraint in Angola and one of the reasons that NMCP continues to rely on PMI-procured commodities. Current legal and regulatory frameworks are not sufficient to guarantee procurement of quality ACTs and RDTs, and the country lacks sufficient capacity to perform QA/QC testing (including a lack of a national reference laboratory). Thus, PMI plans to provide technical assistance to build procurement capacity to procure quality ACTs and RDTs, and perform QA/QC testing in country. *($200,000)*
4. *Continue to support DNME, Inspector General, and the NMCP to improve regulation and monitoring of drug quality for antimalarials*: Building upon previous year's investment, continue to support the regulatory and monitoring systems for quality assurance of antimalarials through development of standard tools, operating procedures, laboratory strengthening and advocacy for regulations *($200,000)*

5. Health system strengthening and capacity building

PMI supports a broad array of health system strengthening activities which cut across intervention areas, such as training of health workers, supply chain management and health information systems strengthening, drug quality monitoring, and NMCP capacity building.

NMCP/PMI objectives
The Angolan NMCP is tasked with planning, supervising, and monitoring malaria activities throughout the country. The Program sets standards, prioritizes use of resources, and tracks progress. A lack of human resources at all levels inhibits progress. Recently, the Angolan decentralization process, whereby municipalities are responsible for a significant portion of planning, budgeting, and financial management of health resources, as well as the cessation of financial support from the Global Fund, have created additional challenges for the NMCP. PMI supports the NMCP to strengthen health systems at all levels in order to improve the malaria program performance and ensure sustainability of PMI's investments. USAID's overall approach to health systems strengthening is through the provision of technical assistance to various levels of the government in the areas of budget and finance, HMIS, human capacity building, and logistics and supply chain management.

Progress since PMI was launched
PMI has worked to strengthen human resources capacity and HMIS in the provinces of Huambo and Luanda through an integrated health systems strengthening activity since 2011. This project works closely with the MoH at the national, provincial, and municipal levels with the goal of improving capacity for service delivery, leadership, management, and supervision skills of health workers to deliver quality care and services. The project supports municipalities to develop their strategies in line with the national health strategy, and also supports the implementation of the National Health System Strategic Information Plan and works to improve effectiveness and efficiency of human resources at the municipal level.

To improve service delivery, PMI has invested in pre-service training of trainers and nursing school teachers for quality improvement and standards-based clinical practices. After the approval of the National Health Development Plan (PNDS) by the Angolan government, USAID and PMI provided significant technical assistance to cost the plan, and supported municipalities in nine provinces to develop municipal health plans and associated budgets in standardized formats and based on epidemiological data.

PMI partners developed a cadre of national, provincial, and municipal supervisors to conduct supportive supervision at health facilities. Support provided by partners included supervision planning and tool development, health facility malaria report verification, and municipal and provincial level malaria reports and database management. In addition, PMI projects promoted active review and discussion of monthly reports with municipal and provincial supervisors to foster analysis for problem identification and explore possible solutions. The focus has been on improving documentation in patient record books so that the quality of the data available for analysis improves.

The Field Epidemiology and Laboratory Training Program (FELTP) began its first cohort in Angola in FY 2012. A collaboration between CDC, the *Agostinho Neto* University, and the MoH, the FELTP trains select health personnel in field epidemiology. Participants acquire skills in data analysis, epidemiologic methods, and use of strategic information to make appropriate health decisions. Annually, PMI supports two students who focus on malaria for their field work; however, in Angola, all of the FELTP students in the program have participated in multiple investigations and responses to malaria outbreaks in different provinces across the country. In 2012 and 2013, the FELTP students participated in multiple suspected and confirmed malaria outbreaks across the county, and developed a "short course" on epidemic investigation and control that is provided at the regional level. The course focuses on timely outbreak detection and response and includes training on the Epi Info® software package. All participants conduct an investigation as a practical exercise in the course and malaria was often the subject chosen. Two students worked on the PMI TES in two provinces, and an FELTP graduate from the first FELTP cohort is taking an active role in leading the implementation of the TES in a third province. Three of the nine members from the first FELTP class have taken prominent positions in the MoH, and one was appointed to be a member of the national emergency response team.

PMI continues to support the Malaria Partners Forum to assist the NMCP in coordinating malaria partners and stakeholders and to track and coordinate all malaria activities. The Forum is responsible for mapping malaria partners as well as creating provincial-level forums to improve coordination amongst partners at lower levels.

Progress during the last 12-18 months
PMI supported the Ministry of Health to develop and finalize a Monitoring and Evaluation Plan for the PNDS, to examine both programmatic and financial progress. The plan includes concrete steps for implementation of M&E activities and will strengthen accountability for program performance and budget execution for PNDS at the central, provincial, and district levels. In order to improve capacity among the Ministry of Health to monitor government spending in particular health areas such as malaria, USAID's integrated health systems strengthening activity is supporting the Health Accounts team to undertake its first health accounts exercise, utilizing the System of Health Accounts 2011 tool modified for the Angolan context. To date, the project has conducted training on the tool and the team will begin the analysis shortly.

PMI's quality improvement program expanded its geographic reach in Luanda and Huambo provinces to work with 44 health facilities in 20 municipalities to build manager's capacity to set standards, monitor quality of services, and use health information systems for decision making. The project trained 129 supervisors on quality improvement, and 164 health providers on standards for malaria services, and updated job aids and electronic tools to meet NMCP guidelines.

Plans and justification
PMI will continue work to build systems and human capacity for managing and monitoring malaria programs. An emphasis will be placed on strengthening the lower levels of the decentralized health system, to ensure that management improvements have a direct impact on the availability and quality of malaria services.

Proposed activities with FY 2016 funding: *($850,000)*

1. Improve health information and supervisory systems for malaria as a component of a cross-cutting systems strengthening approach to build the capacity of provincial supervisors, and improve processes for HMIS systems, supervision of case management, and programmatic planning. Specific activities include: finalize and disseminate the new Malaria in Pregnancy manual; support integrated supervision by NMCP and local health authorities; support the development of municipal operating plans for health; train municipal supervisors on malaria best practices; and improve HMIS capacity at the local level. *($300,000)*

2. Continue to support two students from the FELTP program to focus on malaria activities; additional support for recruitment and retention of students, and outbreak investigation *($200,000)*

3. Work with national and select provincial counterparts to enhance the annual budget formulation process for malaria commodities consistent with the national health budget and municipal health strategies in select provinces. Technical assistance will strengthen medium-term planning for sustainable access to these commodities, among other malaria interventions identified in Angola's sub-sector strategies. PMI will assist the GRA to measure and analyze actual expenditures and link them to the budgeting process, as well as to help determine how provincial and national budgets contribute to national malaria efforts. *($200,000)*

4. Support the Malaria Partner's Forum to assist the NMCP and provinces to coordinate malaria partners. This includes maintenance of the partner database with geographic coverage and scope of activities; quarterly meetings; compilation and collation of partner quarterly reports; website maintenance to ensure resources are used efficiently, minimize duplication, and facilitate sharing of best practices. *($50,000)*

5. Conduct supportive supervision to provincial malaria supervisors to provide them with feedback and assistance as they utilize the skills gained from the previous years' trainings in data collection, analysis, and surveillance. *($100,000)*

Table 8: Health Systems Strengthening Activities

HSS Building Block	Technical Area	Description of Activity
Health Services	MIP	Improve IPTP adherence by health workers through training and dissemination of the updated MIP policy at the municipal and facility levels.
	MIP	Strengthen malaria in pregnancy services at health facilities: training and regular supervision of health providers to improve diagnosis and treatment of malaria in pregnant women
	Case Management	Train trainers at the provincial and municipal level of malaria supervisors on conducting formative supervision; Support municipal malaria supervisors to provide quarterly supervision visits to health facilities.
	Case Management	Train trainers at the provincial and municipal level of laboratory technicians and supervisors on conducting formative supervision.
Health Workforce	Health Systems Strengthening and Capacity Building	Field Epidemiology and Laboratory Training Program
	Health Systems Strengthening and Capacity Building	Build capacity of provincial malaria supervisors in data collection and analysis.
Health Information	Monitoring and Evaluation	Strengthen entomological surveillance systems to improve decision-making, planning, forecasting and program management. Capacity building for staff at the central and provincial level.
	Monitoring and Evaluation	Expand pilot of HMIS database from Huambo to select municipalities in hyperendemic areas.
	Monitoring and Evaluation	Evaluation of HMIS and parallel NMCP recording and reporting system, using abstracted registry data as gold-standard comparison. Provinces selected in order to represent different levels of performance of systems.
	Health Systems Strengthening	Improve health information and supervisory systems for malaria as a component of broader systems strengthening approach.

Essential Medical Products, Vaccines, and Technologies	Pharmaceutical Management	Strengthen pharmaceutical management related to antimalarial drugs including regular supervision and training provincial pharmacists. Strengthen capacity at NMCP to forecast demand and distribute commodities in line with prioritized needs.
	Pharmaceutical Management	Build procurement capacity to procure quality ACTs and RDTs, and perform QA/QC testing in country.
	Pharmaceutical Management	Building upon previous year's investment, continue to support the regulatory and monitoring systems for quality assurance of antimalarials through development of standard tools, operating procedures, laboratory strengthening and advocacy for regulations.
Health Finance	Health Systems Strengthening and Capacity Building	Support MoH and Ministry of Finance with budget and budget monitoring of the National Plan for the Development of the Health Sector, in order to guide procurement at the national and provincial level.
Leadership and Governance	Health Systems Strengthening and Capacity Building	Support to Malaria Partners' Forum secretariat.

6. Behavior change communication

NMCP/PMI objectives
NMCP's objective is that by the end of 2020, at least 80% of caregivers know the cause, signs and symptoms of malaria, and at least one prevention and one treatment measure. BCC activities to increase the uptake of malaria interventions focus on improving ITN use, improving uptake of IPTp, and promoting better understanding of the importance of provision of quality ACTs upon a positive diagnosis with an RDT or microscopy. In order to achieve its objectives, the NMCP and PMI focus BCC investments on interpersonal communication and mass media communications. Interpersonal communication activities include the involvement of local NGOs, faith-based organizations and respected community leaders. The focus for mass media is to use radio as a main vehicle to reach communities in urban and rural areas.

Progress since PMI was launched
The NMCP is currently revising its strategy for IEC/BCC, to provide a framework to guide and coordinate behavior change communication activities for malaria in Angola. The strategy's main goals are to: define roles and responsibilities of all key actors; identify priority issues and gaps; and provide a basis for multi- and bilateral assistance and intersectoral coordination. Overall, the strategy also addresses misconceptions about malaria in Angola and seeks to improve knowledge

in key behaviors essential to achieve sustained malaria control. The strategy covers four main malaria interventions: vector control (IRS, ITNs, and larviciding), case management, IPTp, and epidemic preparedness and response. A BCC working group will be established to help guide, coordinate, and advocate for rigorous evaluation of BCC activities.

With the launch of the universal coverage campaign in 2013, NMCP and partners developed a specific BCC effort focused on improving net use. The BCC activities include municipal health days, house-to-house visits, and radio programs. Angola does not yet have a strong culture of net use; therefore, much work is still needed to promote consistent net use as well as appropriate care. Similar efforts are also needed for case management and MIP.

BCC activities have been coordinated and targeted at the provincial level, given the variation of malaria transmission in Angola. Key messages at the community level, via radio, include promotion of correct net use, importance of malaria prevention during pregnancy, and the importance of prompt diagnosis and treatment of malaria with ACTs. Efforts include multiple channels of communication (radio, personal communication, local drama activities), which are targeted to the areas affected.

The municipal health system revitalization process is intended to improve the quality of existing services and integration of service delivery. Community outreach through municipal health days provides communities with an integrated package of health interventions including ITN distribution, vaccination, de-worming, and other essential services. Thus, the malaria components of BCC before and during these days at the community level is integrated with other health activities and services

Progress during the last 12-18 months

During the past year, the NGO strengthening project has continued to support both mass and interpersonal communication to improve knowledge and change behavior on malaria prevention and care-seeking. Activities included community outreach using face-to-face discussions, drama shows on malaria, and mobile videos; training of health and community workers; radio spots; and printed messages together with those that accompany packaged ITNs and ACTs. Implementation of these activities occurs at various locations, including clinics, homes, religious institutions, schools, and community events.

In FY 2014, the project reached 86,390 people in health facilities (of a target of 88,100) and 99,887 people through community outreach (of a target of 98,440); produced and disseminated 11,538 posters (of a target of 8,900); and aired 469 TV and radio spots aired to target groups (of a target of 1,218).

Between October 1, 2014 and March 31, 2015, the project reached 44,034 people in health facilities (target for FY 2015 is 76,400) and 66,302 people through community outreach (target for FY 2015 is 320,310); produced and disseminated 4,551 posters (target for FY 2015 is 14,670); and aired 604 TV and radio spots aired to target groups (target for FY 2015 is 2,784).

PMI's implementing partner collects and reports on indicators which can be triangulated to determine the impact of the BCC activities on health provider behavior. For example, HMIS data from the facilities where provides have been trained can be analyzed to determine whether providers are in fact administering RDTs prior to treatment, and if they are adhering to the test results. With regard to determining the impact of BCC on desired behavior change in community members, PMI's implementing partner has started tracking behavioral change during FY 2015 and will report the results at the end of the fiscal year.

Within the context of the universal coverage campaign, PMI continues to support BCC to increase ITN usage. In preparation for a new BCC campaign to launch in June 2015 in Bie Province, PMI supported field data collection in Huambo, Bengo, Malanje, and Uige Provinces, a workshop, and development of a communication strategy focused on IPC through church, peer educations, and community meeting points, as well as mass media (mainly radio, with some billboards).

PMI's implementing partner is working with the NMCP to finalize the IEC/BCC strategy develop tools to implement the strategy. The NMCP's capacity to coordinate and monitor all malaria-related BCC activities carried out by the NMCP, provincial governments, implementing partners, and other in-country stakeholders in Angola has been limited. As part of the implementation of the new BCC strategy, PMI is supporting the development of indicators and a tracking system, to better coordinate and measure impact of BCC efforts across the country.

PMI continues to support the National Malaria Partners Forum to ensure effective implementation and coordination of malaria control interventions including BCC focused on the community level and on capacity building at the central level.

Plans and justification
Many Angolans do not have access to public health facilities, thus improving awareness of malaria at the household level is an especially important element of the malaria control strategy. A key component of this strategy is the implementation of iCCM, which is aimed at reaching the underserved population. Once the ADECOS policy is approved and becomes part of the health system, health promotion will be a key component of community health workers' activities.

Under NMCP guidance, PMI plans to focus on the development and roll out of communications materials for mass media and community-based activities, interpersonal communication (IPC), pre-season transmission malaria prevention activities, and case management of malaria. Evidence-based messages focused on a target audience will be used and support will be provided to the NMCP to begin to evaluate specific interventions and actual behavior change.

Proposed activities with FY 2016 funding: ($750,000)
1. Support the roll out of the BCC strategy currently under development by engaging malaria forum members, including civil society groups, international partners, private sector and donors, to establish BCC indicators, track reporting on indicators, and report on the impact of BCC interventions in select provinces. *($100,000)*

2. Develop and conduct training for outreach workers, in order to improve communication skills; produce materials for distribution to incentivize ITN use by identifying and promoting positive behavior. *($250,000)*
3. Undertake BCC at the community and facility levels to promote net use and continue to build a net culture. *($400,000)*
4. Use BCC at the community level to improve prevention of malaria in pregnancy at the community level, through promotion of ANC attendance and education on the importance of ITN use and receiving at least three doses of IPTp (budget incorporated in MIP section).

7. Monitoring and evaluation

NMCP/PMI objectives

Strengthening M&E capacity and using M&E information for data-based decision-making is a priority for PMI and the NMCP. Currently, malaria data in Angola is collected through the HMIS, and by the municipal malaria supervisor through a parallel system. However, HMIS data are unreliable and often conflict with data collected through the parallel system. The NMCP is aware of these limitations and has developed a plan to strengthen M&E, described in the 2011-2015 National Strategic Plan for Malaria Control and the Concept Note submitted to Global Fund. The main M&E objectives of the NMCP's plan are, by 2020:

- To establish an efficient epidemiology surveillance, monitoring and evaluation system in all 18 provinces; and
- To develop capacity to detect and to appropriately respond to epidemics within 2 weeks in 16 epidemic-prone municipalities.

Progress since PMI was launched

Since its launch, PMI has provided training, supervision, data quality checks, and reporting tools to the health facilities at the municipal and provincial levels. In addition, PMI supports the maintenance and the use of a training and supervision database used by municipalities to track staff that have been trained and to track supportive supervision from both the health facility and the municipalities, respectively. These training databases help to minimize duplication and ensure that the staff is provided with the required skill sets.

PMI has supported two MIS (2006/7 and 2011) and is supporting a DHS to be conducted in 2015. The DHS will be conducted in collaboration with the National Institute of Statistics (INE), and will collect data on the primary malaria indicators.

In 2012, PMI and the NMCP supported an evaluation of the impact of malaria control interventions on malaria morbidity and mortality among children under five years of age during 2006–2011. A summary of the findings of this evaluation is described in the Strategy Section.

The 2006/7 MIS provided baseline estimates of malaria control intervention coverage, and the 2011 MIS provided a follow-up after five years of implementing malaria control interventions.

PMI Angola is at the forefront of monitoring malaria parasite resistance to artemisinin-based combination therapies, including therapeutic efficacy surveys in 2013 and 2015 [see Case Management Section for more detail].

In 2013, an evaluation of the Malaria Early Warning System (MEWS) was performed in Cuando Cubango, an epidemic-prone province. This evaluation showed the presence of inconsistent stocks of diagnostic supplies, errors in patient registries and report forms, and lack of staff's ability to conduct the system's activities at the facility and municipal levels. Several recommendations were made to improve the system, and PMI continues to work with the NMCP on incorporating these recommendations into future programming.

Progress during the last 12-18 months

Enhanced Epidemiological Surveillance: In 2014, together with the NMCP and its implementing partner, PMI implemented an enhanced epidemiologic surveillance activity in nine health units in five municipalities across the three PMI-targeted provinces: Huambo and Bailundo (Huambo Province), Lubango, (Huila Province), and Kwanhama and Namacunde (Cunene Province). Findings of this activity demonstrated a lack of interest in surveillance by health facilities' directors, poor standard data collection, non-compliance to malaria testing, and stockouts of RDTs and ACTs. As a result, PMI-trained health facility staff and conducted supervisory visits to ensure malaria data collection and reporting processes were being followed.

Training and Capacity Building: In 2014, PMI supported a 6-week visit of the NMCP official responsible for laboratory monitoring and supervision, to the CDC, Atlanta, for advanced training in molecular biology techniques for malaria diagnosis, including Real-Time PCR, Sanger sequencing, and microsatellite genotyping analysis.

Antimalarial availability monitoring: PMI continues to support bi-annual end-use verification surveys as part of the plan to improve the supply chain management system. The most recent EUV conducted November/December 2014 visited 42 health facilities and warehouses from 5 (of 18) provinces. Results of this survey showed that RDT stockouts were high on the day of the visit at 50%, but stockouts for 3 or more days in the last 3 months were lower at 13%. In addition, 43% of health facilities did not have any presentation of ACTs on the day of visit.

Entomological Surveillance: Entomological surveillance, including the collection of basic core entomological indicators such as the presence and identification of the vector species and insecticide susceptibility status, is an essential component of PMI vector control activities in Angola. Refer to the Vector Control section for more details

Therapeutic Efficacy Survey: The NMCP, with support from CDC, WHO and PMI, successfully launched the 2015 Therapeutic Efficacy Survey in the provinces of Benguela, Zaire, and Lunda Sul in early 2015. The objective of the 2015 TES is to measure the efficacy of three antimalarials (artemether-lumefantrine, artesunate-amodiaquine and dihydroartemisinin-piperaquine) and will be essential to monitor the continuing efficacy of artemisinin-combination therapy for falciparum malaria in Angola.

ITN Durability Monitoring: Results of a PMI-supported 2011-2013 ITN durability monitoring study were presented to the NMCP in May 2015. Of the nets found in the households after two years of use, approximately 20% were classified as torn using the WHO classification. In the first year, most of the nets not found were not for reasons of net damage. More nets were not found in the houses visited due to destruction after two years of use. Of the nets found in the households after two years of use, approximately 20% did not protect the users adequately using the WHO proportional hole index.

Table 9. Monitoring and Evaluation Data Sources

Data Source	Survey Activities	Year								
		2010	2011	2012	2013	2014	2015	2016	2017	2018
National-level Household surveys	Demographic Health Survey (DHS)						X			
	Malaria Indicator Survey (MIS)		X							X
Health Facility and Other Surveys	Health facility survey							X*		
	EUV survey	X	X	X	X	X	X	X	X	X
Malaria Surveillance and Routine System Support	Support to malaria surveillance system	X	X	X	X	X	X	X	X	X
	Support to parallel routine malaria info system? (for GF or other reporting)	X	X	X	X	X	X	X	X	X
	Support to HMIS	X	X	X	X	X	X	X	X	X
Therapeutic Efficacy monitoring	In vivo efficacy testing				X		X		X	
Entomology	Entomological surveillance and resistance monitoring	X		X	X	X	X	X	X	X
Other malaria-related evaluations	Net durability monitoring		X	X	X					
Other Data Sources	Malaria Impact Evaluation			X		X				

*Not PMI-funded
* The health facility survey is planned to start in November 2015.

Plans and justification

With FY 2016 funding, PMI will continue to support malaria M&E within the framework of the National Malaria M&E Plan described in the National Strategic Plan for Malaria Control (2011-2015). Available funding will be targeted towards improving the country's M&E capacity, data quality assurance, and using data for decision making.

Proposed activities with FY 2016 funding: ($815,000)

1. Continue bi-annual End Use Verification/monitoring of commodity availability and use at health facility level. *($150,000)*

2. Support 2 CDC TDYs to provide M&E assistance to the NMCP and in-country partners, including supporting the ITN durability monitoring study. *($20,000)*

3. Expand pilot of HMIS database from Huambo to select municipalities in hyperendemic areas. *($300,000)*

4. According with WHO guidelines, therapeutic efficacy studies should be conducted every 2-3 years. In 2017, PMI will support a third TES in Angola, to be conducted in the 3 sites established in 2015 (Benguela, Zaire, and Lunda Sul). *($250,000)*

5. Support 2 CDC TDY visits to provide training and supervision during the TES, and purchase of specialized supplies not available locally. *($30,000)*

6. Evaluation of HMIS and parallel NMCP recording and reporting system, using abstracted registry data as gold-standard comparison. Provinces, potentially Huambo and Cabinda, will be selected in order to represent different levels of performance of systems. *($65,000)*

8. Operational research

As part of Angola's national strategic plan, there is a priority list in that guides decisions on operational research (OR). However, to date, there has not been much operational research undertaken in Angola.

Since the end of the war, Angola has been a magnet for Asian migrants seeking economic opportunities, and the size of the population of Southeast Asian migrants in Angola is estimated to be one of the largest concentrations of Asians in Africa. Because most of these migrants come from malaria endemic and drug-resistant areas, PMI proposes to support a qualitative study among the Southeast Asia migrant worker population, in an effort to understand their malaria healthcare-seeking behavior and prevention practices. *($75,000)*

Table 10. PMI-funded Operational Research Studies

Planned OR Studies FY 2016			
Title	**Start date (est.)**	**End date (est.)**	**Budget**
Qualitative Study on malaria healthcare-seeking behavior and prevention practices among the Southeast Asia migrant workers	October 2016	December 2016	$75,000

9. Staffing and administration

Two health professionals serve as resident advisors to oversee PMI in Angola, one representing CDC and one representing USAID. In addition, one or more Foreign Service Nationals (FSNs) work as part of the PMI team. All PMI staff members are part of a single interagency team led by the USAID Mission Director or his/her designee in country. The PMI team shares responsibility for development and implementation of PMI strategies and work plans, coordination with national authorities, managing collaborating agencies and supervising day-to-day activities. Candidates for resident advisor positions (whether initial hires or replacements) will be evaluated and/or interviewed jointly by USAID and CDC, and both agencies will be involved in hiring decisions, with the final decision made by the individual agency.

The PMI professional staff work together to oversee all technical and administrative aspects of the PMI, including finalizing details of the project design, implementing malaria prevention and treatment activities, monitoring and evaluation of outcomes and impact, reporting of results, and providing guidance to PMI partners.

The PMI lead in country is the USAID Mission Director. The day-to-day lead for PMI is delegated to the USAID General Development Officer and thus the two PMI resident advisors, one from USAID and one from CDC, report to the USAID General Development Officer for day-to-day leadership, and work together as a part of a single interagency team. The technical expertise housed in Atlanta and Washington guides PMI programmatic efforts.

The two PMI resident advisors are based within the USAID health office and are expected to spend approximately half their time sitting with and providing technical assistance to the national malaria control programs and partners.

Locally-hired staff to support PMI activities either in Ministries or in USAID will be approved by the USAID Mission Director. Because of the need to adhere to specific country policies and USAID accounting regulations, any transfer of PMI funds directly to Ministries or host governments will need to be approved by the USAID Mission Director and Controller, in addition to the U.S. Global Malaria Coordinator.

Proposed activities with FY 2016 funding: ($2,910,000)
- USAID/PMI staffing: Support to salaries, benefits, and ICASS for 1 PSC or TCN (Resident Advisor) and 2 support staff (FSNs). *($1,300,000)*
- USAID admin/ PD&L: *($540,000)*
- CDC IAA admin: *($1,070,000)*

Table 1: Budget Breakdown by Mechanism

President's Malaria Initiative – Angola

Planned Malaria Obligations for FY 2016

Mechanism	Geographic Area	Activity	Mechanism Budget ($)	%
TBD - Supply Chain Contract	Hyperendemic provinces (such as Uige,Cuanza Norte, Lunda Norte, Lunda Sul, Malanje, Zaire)/ Nationwide	Procurement of ITNs; Transportation of ITNs from central to provincial levels Procurement of laboratory supplies for microscopy and PCR; Procurement of RDTs; Procurement of ACTs; Procurement of injectable artesunate for treatment of severe malaria; Procurement of intramuscular artemether (IM) for treatment of severe malaria; Technical assistance and support for import, clearance, storage, distribution and management of RDT and ACT commodities	$13,385,000	50%
TBD - Projecto de Angolanizacao Bilateral/Health capacity building	Hyperendemic provinces (such as Uige,Cuanza Norte, Lunda Norte, Lunda Sul, Malanje, Zaire)/ Nationwide/ Uige and 1 more province (TBD)	Routine distribution of ITNs and strenghtening of distribution system; Training and support in the dissemination of current policy to provide at least three doses of SP at the municipal and facility levels; Strengthen malaria in pregnancy services at health facilities; Strengthen malaria case management; Training and supervision on laboratory diagnosis (microscopy) and quality control; Expand support to iCCM/ADECOS activity Build capacity of provincial malaria supervisors in data collection and analysis; Evaluation of routine malaria recording and reporting systems.	$6,400,000	24%

TBD - BCC project	Hyperendemic provinces (such as Uige,Cuanza Norte, Lunda Norte, Lunda Sul, Malanje, Zaire)/ Nationwide TBD (Uige and 1 other province)	IEC/BCC for malaria in pregnancy at the community level; Support to Malaria Partners' Forum secretariat; Develop national BCC strategy, including prevention (ITNs and malaria in pregnancy) and case management; Training of ADECOS on malaria prevention at the community level (e.g., communication strategies for improving net use culture, early diagnosis and treatment, and IPTp) BCC campaign to promote net use and care and repair.	$900,000	3%
VectorWorks	Nationwide	TA to explore alternative mechanisms to increase ownership and use of ITNs	$270,000	1%
IRS 2 TO6	Huila, Cunene, Huambo, Uige, Malange, Benguela, Namibe, Zaire, Luanda, Lunda Sul, and Lunda Norte	Entomological surveillance; PCR testing of mosquitoes	$710,000	3%
MSH/SIAPS	Nationwide and select provinces	Strengthen Ministry of Health antimalarial drug management system; Survey of availability of malaria commodities at the health facility level (End use verification); Strengthen Ministry of Health QA/QC systems and capacity.	$1,000,000	4%
U.S. Pharmacopoeia	Nationwide	Continue to support DNME, Inspector General, and the NMCP to improve regulation and monitoring of drug quality for antimalarials	$200,000	1%
JHPEIGO /SASH	Select hyperendeic provinces (e.g., Zaire, Uige)	Facilitate malaria program implementation and health systems strengthening in collaboration with NMCP; Epidemiological surveillance	$600,000	2%
Abt Associates/Ampla Saude	Nationwide	Support MoH and Ministry of Finance with budget and budget monitoring of the National Plan for the Development of the Health Sector	$200,000	1%

CDC	Nationwide/ Benguela, Lunda Sul, Zaire	Technical assistance for entomologic monitoring and insecticide resistance testing; Field Epidemiology and Laboratory Training Program; Technical support for strengthening M&E; Technical support for therapeutic efficacy monitoring and select supplies.	$290,000	1%
TBD	TBD	Technical assistance to assist in continuation and sustainable transition of private sector case management services activity	$60,000	0%
TBD	Lunda Sul, Lunda Norte	Assessment of malaria healthcare seeking and prevention practices among Southeast Asian migrant workers	$75,000	0%
Staffing and Administration	Nationwide	USAID and CDC staffing and admin	$2,910,000	11%
Total			**$27,000,000**	**100%**

Table 2: Budget Breakdown by Activity

President's Malaria Initiative – Angola

Planned Malaria Obligations for FY 2016

Proposed Activity	Mechanism	Budget		Geographic Area	Description
		Total $	Commodity $		
PREVENTIVE ACTIVITIES					
Insecticide-treated Nets					
Procurement of ITNs	TBD - Supply Chain Contract	$5,475,000	$5,475,000	Hyperendemic provinces (such as Uige, Cuanza Norte, Lunda Norte, Lunda Sul, Malanje, Zaire)	Procure approximately 1.5 million ITNs
Transportation of ITNs from central to provincial levels	TBD - Supply Chain Contract	$2,175,000		Hyperendemic provinces (such as Uige, Cuanza Norte, Lunda Norte, Lunda Sul, Malanje, Zaire)	Distribution of ITNs from the central level to select provinces
Routine distribution of ITNs and strengthening of distribution system.	TBD - *Projecto de Angolanizacao* Bilateral/Health capacity building	$1,885,000		Hyperendemic provinces (such as Uige, Cuanza Norte, Lunda Norte, Lunda Sul, Malanje, Zaire)	Routine distribution of ITNs through ANC for pregnant women and EPI for children under five, and potentially additional distribution mechanism(s). Also includes monitoring of distribution to end users.

Activity	Mechanism	Amount	Amount	Location	Description
TA to implement strategy to increase ownership and use of ITNs	VectorWorks	$270,000		Nationwide	In follow up to the 2014 NetCalc workshop and planned technical assistance with FY 2015 funds, provide technical assistance to work with in-country stakeholders to improve continuous distribution of ITNs.
SUBTOTAL ITNs		**$9,805,000**	**$5,475,000**		
Entomological Monitoring					
Entomological surveillance	IRS 2 TO6	$650,000		Huila, Cunene, Huambo, Uige, Malange, Benguela, Namibe, Zaire, Luanda, Lunda Sul, and Lunda Norte	Routine entomologic monitoring (including in former IRS areas), susceptibility studies, vector density. Capacity building for central and provincial staff. Work in provinces where 2015 susceptibility study was undertaken as well as Lunda Sul and Lunda Norte.
Entomological laboratory testing of mosquitoes	IRS 2 TO6	$60,000		Nationwide	PCR processing of mosquitoes from Angola until the capacity in Angola is sufficient for local processing; a portion of this funding will be used to purchase PCR supplies
Technical assistance for entomologic monitoring and insecticide resistance testing	CDC	$40,000		Nationwide	Technical assistance visits for entomologic monitoring and resistance testing in NMCP; support for specific reagents and other laboratory diagnostic materials
SUBTOTAL Entomological Monitoring		**$750,000**	**$0**		
Malaria in Pregnancy					

Activity	Funding Source	Amount	Amount	Location	Notes
Training and support in the dissemination of current policy to provide at least three doses of SP at the municipal and facility levels.	*TBD - Projecto de Angolanizacao Bilateral/Health capacity building*	$100,000		Hyperendemic provinces (such as Uige,Cuanza Norte, Lunda Norte, Lunda Sul, Malanje, Zaire)	
IEC/BCC for malaria in pregnancy at the community level	TBD - BCC project	$100,000		Hyperendemic provinces (such as Uige,Cuanza Norte, Lunda Norte, Lunda Sul, Malanje, Zaire)	
Strengthen malaria in pregnancy services at health facilities	*TBD - Projecto de Angolanizacao Bilateral/Health capacity building*	$200,000		Hyperendemic provinces (such as Uige,Cuanza Norte, Lunda Norte, Lunda Sul, Malanje, Zaire)	
Subtotal Malaria in Pregnancy		$400,000	$0		
SUBTOTAL PREVENTIVE		$10,955,000	$5,475,000		
CASE MANAGEMENT					
Diagnosis and Treatment					
Procurement of laboratory supplies for microscopy and PCR	TBD - Supply Chain Contract	$50,000	$50,000	Nationwide	Procurement of laboratory diagnostic reagents and supplies
Procurement of RDTs	TBD - Supply Chain Contract	$3,120,000	$3,120,000	Select provinces (Bengo, Bié, Cabinda, Kuanza Norte, Kuanza Sul, Lunda Norte, Lunda Sul, Malange, Uíge, Zaire)	Procurement of 5,880,000 RDTs for the public sector and private sector

Procurement of ACTs	TBD - Supply Chain Contract	$2,065,000	$2,065,000	Select provinces (Bengo, Bié, Cabinda, Kuanza Norte, Kuanza Sul, Lunda Sul, Lunda Sul, Malange, Uige, Zaire)	Procurement of 3,300,000 treatments of AS-AQ for the public sector
Procurement of injectable artesunate for treatment of severe malaria	TBD - Supply Chain Contract	$60,000	$60,000	Nationwide	Procurement of approximately 30,000 treatments of severe malaria; assume 6% of 3M malaria cases are severe
Procurement of intramuscular artemether (IM) for treatment of severe malaria	TBD - Supply Chain Contract	$140,000	$140,000	Nationwide	Procurement of approximately 70,000 treatments of severe malaria; assume 6% of 3M malaria cases are severe
Strengthen malaria case management	TBD - *Projecto de Angolanizacao* Bilateral/Health capacity building	$3,000,000		Nationwide for training; support for supervision in priority hyperendemic provinces (such as Uige, Cuanza Norte, Lunda Norte, Lunda Sul, Malanje, Zaire)	Training, support supervision for provincial and health facility health workers to improve malaria case management. Include: (1) Training of trainers at the provincial and municipal level of malaria supervisors on conducting formative supervision; (2) support to municipal level (malaria supervisors) to provide regular supervision visits to health facilities on a quarterly basis.
Training and supervision on laboratory diagnosis (microscopy) and quality control	TBD - *Projecto de Angolanizacao* Bilateral/Health capacity building	$600,000		Nationwide for training; support for supervision in priority hyperendemic provinces (such as Uige, Cuanza Norte, Lunda Norte, Lunda Sul, Malanje, Zaire)	Training, and support supervision for provincial and municipal laboratory technicians and supervisors to improve malaria diagnostics in the laboratory, i.e., Training of trainers at the provincial and municipal level of laboratory technicians and supervisors on conducting formative supervision

61

Activity	Partner	Budget	Location	Description
Expand support to iCCM/ADECOS activity	TBD - *Projecto de Angolanizacao* Bilateral/Health capacity building	$200,000	Uige and 1 more province (TBD)	Continue to support the GRA's iCCM initiative with ADECOS (community health workers) in selected municipalities. PMI will provide RDTs and ACTs; the MoH will provide commodities for the other diseases included in the care package (ex. pneumonia, diarrhea)
Technical assistance to assist in continuation and sustainable transition of private sector case management services activity	TBD	$60,000	TBD	Prepare for potential Global Fund support for expansion of private sector case management services pilot
Subtotal Diagnosis and Treatment		$9,295,000	$5,435,000	
Pharmaceutical Management				
Technical assistance and support for import, clearance, storage, distribution and management of RDT and ACT commodities	TBD - Supply Chain Contract	$300,000	Nationwide	Provide assistance in the distribution from port, and storage through customs, and down through provincial level
Strengthen Ministry of Health antimalarial drug management system	MSH/SIAPS	$650,000	Nationwide	Strengthen pharmaceutical management related to antimalarial drugs including regular supervision, provincial training of pharmacist, help with printing of supply chain management forms. Strengthen capacity at NMCP to forecast demand and distribute commodities in line with prioritized needs

Activity	Implementer	Amount		Location	Description
Strengthen Ministry of Health QA/QC systems and capacity	MSH/SIAPS	$200,000		Nationwide level (Luanda) and select provinces	Build procurement capacity to procure quality ACTs and RDTs, and perform QA/QC testing in country
Continue to support DNME, Inspector General, and the NMCP to improve regulation and monitoring of drug quality for antimalarials	U.S. Pharmacopoeia	$200,000		Nationwide	Building upon previous year's investment, continue to support the regulatory and monitoring systems for quality assurance of antimalarials through development of standard tools, operating procedures, laboratory strengthening and advocacy for regulations
Subtotal Pharmaceutical Management		$1,350,000	$0		
SUBTOTAL CASE MANAGEMENT		$10,645,000	$5,435,000		
HEALTH SYSTEM STRENGTHENING / CAPACITY BUILDING					
Facilitate malaria program implementation and health systems strengthening in collaboration with NMCP	JHPEIGO /SASH	$300,000		Select hyperendeic provinces (e.g., Zaire, Uige)	Contribute to malaria program implementation as part of larger health systems strengthening initiative within MoH.
Field Epidemiology and Laboratory Training Program	CDC	$200,000		Nationwide	Support two students in the field epidemiology and laboratory training program to focus on malaria; additional funds to ensure recruitment/retention and supporting training in the epidemiologic monitoring sites (short course in epidemiology training)

63

Activity	Partner/Project	Cost	Location	Description
Support MoH and Ministry of Finance with budget and budget monitoring of the National Plan for the Development of the Health Sector	Abt Associates/Ampla Saude	$200,000	Nationwide	Technical assistance for cost analyses, bottleneck analyses and monitoring of the PNDS and NMCP strategy
Support to Malaria Partners' Forum secretariat	TBD - BCC project	$50,000	Nationwide	Continued support to National Malaria Partners' Forum
Build capacity of provincial malaria supervisors in data collection and analysis	TBD - *Projecto de Angolanizacao* Bilateral/Health capacity building	$100,000	Hyperendemic provinces (such as Uige, Cuanza Norte, Lunda Norte, Lunda Sul, Malanje, Zaire)	Field visits to conduct supportive supervision
Subtotal Health System Strengthening		$850,000		
BEHAVIOR CHANGE AND COMMUNICATION				
Develop national BCC strategy, including prevention (ITNs and malaria in pregnancy) and case management	TBD - BCC project	$100,000	Nationwide	Develop BCC strategy with appropriate, targeting messages for all level of the system
Training of ADECOS on malaria prevention at the community level (e.g., communication strategies for improving net use culture, early diagnosis and treatment, and IPTp)	TBD - BCC project	$250,000	TBD (Uige and 1 other province)	Includes developing and conducting training for outreach workers, improving communication skills, materials for distribution to incentivize ITN use by identifying and promoting positive behavior

64

Activity	Partner	Cost		Location	Description
BCC campaign to promote net use and care and repair	TBD - BCC project	$400,000		Hyperendemic provinces (such as Lunda Norte, Lunda Sul, Kwanza Norte, Malanje, Zaire)	BCC at the community and facility levels to promote net use and continue to build a net culture
SUBTOTAL BCC		**$750,000**	**$0**		
MONITORING AND EVALUATION					
Survey of availability of malaria commodities at the health facility level (End use verification)	MSH/SIAPS	$150,000		Nationwide	At least biannual monitoring of commodity availability and use at health facility level
Technical support for strengthening M&E	CDC	$20,000		Nationwide	Two TDY visits to provide assistance to in-country partners for M&E (including durability monitoring)
Epidemiological surveillance	JHPEIGO /SASH	$300,000		TBD (Select municipalities in hyperendemic provinces)	Expand pilot of HMIS database from Huambo to select municipalities in hyperendemic areas
Therapeutic efficacy monitoring	TBD - *Projecto de Angolanizacao* Bilateral/Health capacity building	$250,000		Benguela, Lunda Sul, Zaire	Therapeutic efficacy studies in the three established sites from 2015 (Benguela, Zaire, and Lunda Sul)
Technical support for therapeutic efficacy monitoring and select supplies	CDC	$30,000	$10,000	Benguela, Lunda Sul, Zaire	Two CDC TDY visits to provide training and supervision during the TES, and purchase of specialized supplies not available locally

Activity		Amount		Location	Description
Evaluation of routine malaria recording and reporting systems	TBD - *Projecto de Angolanizacao* Bilateral/Health capacity building	$65,000		TBD (potentially Huambo, Cabinda)	Evaluation of HMIS and parallel NMCP recording and reporting system, using abstracted registry data as gold-standard comparison. Provinces selected in order to represent different levels of performance of systems.
SUBTOTAL M&E		**$815,000**	**$10,000**		
OPERATIONAL RESEARCH					
Assessment of malaria healthcare seeking and prevention practices among Southeast Asian migrant workers	TBD	$75,000		Lunda Sul, Lunda Norte	Qualitative study of malaria healthseeking behavior and prevention practices in Southeast Asia migrant worker population. Many of these workers come from malaria endemic and drug-resistant areas. The size of the population in Angola is estimated to be 400,000, considered to be the largest concentrated population in Africa.
SUBTOTAL OR		**$75,000**	**$0**		
IN-COUNTRY STAFFING AND ADMINISTRATION					
Staffing and Administration	USAID/PMI staffing	$1,300,000		Nationwide	Support to salaries, benefits, and ICASS for 1 PSC or TCN (Resident Advisor) and 2 support staff (FSNs)
	USAID admin/ PD&L	$540,000		Nationwide	2% for Mission admin and PD&L
	CDC IAA admin	$1,070,000		Nationwide	
SUBTOTAL IN-COUNTRY STAFFING		**$2,910,000**	**$0**		
GRAND TOTAL		**$27,000,000**	**$10,920,000**